Eagles of Mitsubishi

Eagles of Mitsubishi

The Story of the

ZERO FIGHTER

by Jiro Horikoshi

Translated by Shojiro Shindo
and Harold N. Wantiez

UNIVERSITY OF WASHINGTON PRESS

Originally published in Japanese in 1970 by Kappa Books
(Kobunsha Co., Ltd.), Tokyo, Japan

English translation and Translators' Preface © 1981
by the University of Washington Press

Printed in the United States of America

Library of Congress Cataloging in Publication Data

Horikoshi, Jirō.
    Eagles of Mitsubishi.
    Translation of Zerosen.
    1. Zero (Fighter planes) I. Title.
UG1242.F5H6813   358.4'3   80–29217
ISBN 0–295–95826–X

Translators' Preface

As the fortieth anniversary of the Pearl Harbor attack approaches, it is timely that the complete story of the development of the Zero fighter, which enabled Japan to commence hostilities in the Pacific theater, be made available to readers in the Western world. For this reason we have translated, to the best of our abilities, the story of the Zero, as originally written by its chief designer, Dr. Jiro Horikoshi, and published in Japan during 1970. We believe our translation is an accurate rendition of the Japanese manuscript; in a few instances we have added translators' footnotes where we disagree with the data presented or wish to clarify a point, but it remains Dr. Horikoshi's story. In this preface we wish to add a few thoughts of our own which may give the reader some insight into the origins of the Pacific war and why the Allied powers were caught unawares.

Until Commodore Perry's visit in 1853, Japan was a closed country, allowing no one to enter or leave her shores. This policy had been in effect for several hundred years and was established to keep out Western ideas and religions. A small foreign trading mission in Nagasaki harbor was the only Japanese connection with the West and, consequently, the industrialization of Japan did not begin until the 1880s when Emperor Meiji realized the backward condition of his country and ordered his subjects to catch up with the rest of the world. Young Japanese students were sent to other countries to study and learn modern technology; products were imported, disassembled, studied, and often exactly duplicated. Because of this, Japan was branded a copyist by other nations, which conveniently forgot that they had done the same thing during their industrial gestation period. With growing experience and improved industrial facilities, Japan soon developed original ideas and products, but this went largely unnoticed or ignored by the West. Americans also failed to take notice of the relationship between the Japanese worker and his employer. Far from being at each other's throat, both labor and management were keenly interested in their mutual welfare and strove to cooperate. Modern industrial Japan shows the wisdom of this philosophy.

The origins of World War II were complex and had their roots in the settlement of World War I. Japan emerged from the first world conflict on the side of the Allies, but soon became an economic competitor with the United States. Eventually, after the economic collapse of 1929, the United States attempted to eliminate the competition by banning the importation of Japanese goods. But economics was only one of the primary causes of World War II; among others we can also list mutual fear and misunderstanding.

We sincerely hope the readers of this English-language edition will gain a better understanding of the Japanese way of life as it was before and during World War II; in particular the employee's attitude toward his job and family and the employer's attitude toward his workers. Dr. Horikoshi's motivation in writing the original text was to encourage and stimulate the young people of this and future generations to strive for excellence in everything they do. Perhaps this English-language edition may further help to bridge the gap of misunderstanding which still exists in this imperfect world.

Translators' Acknowledgments

The translation of a book is not an easy matter; the difficulties are compounded when the translators are separated by many thousands of miles from the author. We were fortunate, however, in having the assistance of Mr. Tsuneo Noguchi of Nihon University as our liaison in Japan with Dr. Jiro Horikoshi. Through Mr. Noguchi's efforts, we were able to overcome many formidable obstacles. Despite health problems, Dr. Horikoshi enthusiastically reviewed our manuscript and offered several valuable suggestions. We also gratefully acknowledge the cooperation of the Kobunsha Co., Ltd., which published the original Japanese edition. We express our sincere thanks to Dr. Horikoshi, Mr. Noguchi, and the Kobunsha Co., Ltd., for their cooperation. Thanks are also owed to the members of our families, especially our wives, Mrs. Kazumi Shindo and Mrs. Yoshiko Wantiez, for their encouragement and support during our long and arduous task.

We wish to dedicate this English-language edition to the memory of all airmen who gave their lives in the service of their countries during World War II. We also wish to make a special dedication to the memory of Mr. Mamoru Shindo and Mr. C. E. Swain.

December 1980   Shojiro Shindo
                                               Harold N. Wantiez

Author's Preface

Zero fighter was the name given to the Type Zero Carrier-Based (or Deck-Landing) Fighter. This aircraft was the mainstay of the Japanese Navy and fought from the beginning to the end of World War II. As the Zero's chief designer, I was involved in its development since its inception in 1937. Over twenty-five years have passed since the end of the war and, during that time, Japan has made a miraculous economic recovery. The war is now mentioned only rarely, perhaps because of the natural desire shared by most Japanese people to forget the days of the frightening dreams. But despite the unpleasant memories, people both in and outside Japan still talk about the Zero fighter. Several years ago a Zero was returned to Japan for restoration after its crumbled wreckage was discovered on one of the southern islands. I have also been informed that efforts are under way in Canada to restore three Zeros.[1]

Why does the legend of the Zero survive to this day in the minds of so many people? The late Commander Eiichi Iwaya, who was in charge of the fighter engineering section at the Naval Aeronautics Headquarters, stated in his postwar book, "If there is any respect left in foreigners' minds for the people of Japan, who lost everything in the

1. Translators' note: One flying Zero was assembled from the parts of three wrecked airframes and is now housed at the Marine Corps Museum in Quantico, Virginia.

ix

war, it should be for those who produced and were able to command Zero fighters as they reigned over two oceans." Perhaps it is not in good taste for me to say this, but if, as some people believe, Japanese people excel only in imitating and making small gadgets, then the Zero did not exist. The Zero was of Japanese blood, and its design reflects our philosophy of independent thinking. We were trying to surpass the rest of the world's technology, not just catch up to it. That was the goal of the Zero I designed. Therein might lie the reason for the survival of the Zero legend.

The Navy's requirements for this fighter were severe and at first appeared to be impossible. We in the design group strove to make the impossible possible. In considering the development of the Zero, we must always remember the sacrifice made by two brave Navy test pilots who were lost during the flight test program, and also the cooperation of many other people and associated industries. We must also thank those Japanese pioneers who learned the technologies of the advanced nations and, in turn, gave them to us along with their own innovations. Also, we owe thanks to the Navy and our own company, Mitsubishi, for providing a suitable environment and a project worthy of our best efforts. Surely, in a larger sense, the Zero was the product of the efforts and ideas of all Japanese of those times and not just those connected with the design.

Today, although Japanese technology is said to be advancing daily, our industrial history is very short compared to the two-hundred-year experience of America and Europe. In addition, the lack of natural resources in Japan is a very serious problem. Also, the level of technology and the number of people who support it are far from adequate. I wrote this book with the hope that the young people of today would strive hard with pride, courage, and sincerity to build and better the future of Japan in every field and not just in the field of technology.

At the same time, I would like to add that to accomplish a great task, one must contend with hardships and worries that are both formidable and long-standing. The following was written by Igor Sikorsky, the father of the helicopter, whom I greatly admire: "The life of a man who deeply devotes himself to his work is a repetition of more violent ups and downs than those of an ordinary man." I will be very happy if other people conclude that the short periods of enjoyment, which appear between the ups and downs in their lives, give them the feeling that their lives are worth living.

March 1970 Jiro Horikoshi

To the English-language Edition

I am extremely pleased to see this English translation of my book and know that readers in the Western world can now learn how the Zero was conceived and developed. There have been many stories and rumors concerning the evolution of the Zero; my book is as accurate as my memory will allow, and should settle any controversies.

It has been many years since the end of the Pacific war. Today, America and Japan are friends and allies, and I believe this friendship will continue for many years to come. I sincerely hope this English-language edition of the story of the Zero fighter will be of interest and value to our friends in the West.

December 1980 Jiro Horikoshi

Contents

Illustrations

Eagles of Mitsubishi

Introduction

It happened on 6 October 1937. I had reported for work a little early that day, as we were working on details for fighters already in production. In the ten years since I had joined Mitsubishi Heavy Industries, the Nagoya aircraft manufacturing plant had been my place of work. Although we had already designed several fighter aircraft and had gained considerable experience, I had no idea of the difficult task which would be handed to me that unforgettable day.

I entered the building, after glancing at the clock, and went to the design room located on the third floor. There I saw Mr. Hattori, the chief of the design section, and about half of the designers. He anxiously called me to his desk, as though he had been waiting, and said, "It is finally here." Glancing down, I saw a document printed in Japanese characters. It was titled "Planning Requirements for the Prototype 12 Carrier-Based Fighter." I thought to myself, "Here it comes." It was customary, in those days, for the Navy to issue a planning requirements document when it sponsored the development of a new fighter aircraft by private industry. In May 1937 a preliminary planning document for the Prototype 12 fighter had been issued to us at Mitsubishi, and I had participated in conferences at the Naval Aeronautics Headquarters concerning this new design.[1]

---

1. Translators' note: Prototype 12 was the name given to the experimental fighter whose specifications were released in 1937, which was also the year Showa 12 in Japan, the twelfth year of the reign of the present emperor. In the West, Japanese prototypes are more commonly known as the 7 shi, 9 shi, 12 shi, etc.—shi being the abbreviation for *shisaku*, meaning "experimental."

3

The new fighter I had been planning was an improvement over existing designs, and I was confident I could handle the design of the Prototype 12. However, when I looked at the final requirements I could not believe my eyes. They were far more demanding than what I had expected and seemed impossible to meet. If this airplane could be built, it certainly would be superior to the rest of the world's fighters. To me the specifications sounded like an aviator's selfish wish. There were nearly twenty items in all; only a few are listed here:

Purpose: Escort fighter with dogfight performance superior to that of its opponents. It also must be an interceptor capable of destroying enemy attackers.

Dimensions: Wing span must be less than 12 meters.

Maximum Speed: More than 500 km/hr at 4,000 meters altitude.

Time to Climb: Less than 3.5 minutes to 3,000 meters altitude.

Endurance: At full power using internal fuel only, 1.2 to 1.5 hours at 3,000 meters altitude. In an overload condition using both internal and external fuel tanks, 1.5 to 2.0 hours. At economic cruising speed, 6 to 8 hours.[2]

Takeoff Field Length: Less than 70 meters with a head wind of 12 m/sec, to be able to take off from a carrier deck. Approximately 2.5 times the 70-meter distance for a no-wind condition.

Dogfight Performance: Not less than the Type 96 carrier-based fighter (Model 2–1).

Armament: Two 20-mm cannons. Two 7.7-mm machine guns.

Communications Equipment: Radio and full direction-finding equipment.

Power plant: Mitsubishi Zuisei Type 13 engine (maximum 875 hp at 3,600 meters altitude) or the Mitsubishi Kinsei Type 46 engine (maximum 1,070 hp at 4,200 meters altitude).

2. Translators' note: Dr. Horikoshi's original book did not list range. It was approximately 1,870 kilometers with a normal load and 3,110 kilometers with a drop-tank.

The Background Which Produced Such Severe Requirements

The Navy told us to produce such a fighter. I dropped into my chair as I tossed the document on my desk. Just glancing at the requirements was enough to make me feel gloomy. This aircraft must be an escort fighter and at the same time it must also be an interceptor. An escort fighter has the duty of protecting friendly bombers when they penetrate enemy airspace. It must have long range as well as adequate speed and performance in order to oppose enemy fighters. On the other hand, the interceptor's duties are to intercept and destroy enemy aircraft. This naturally requires a high rate of climb, adequate armament and equipment, and dogfight performance superior to that of the enemy escort fighters.

The range and performance requirements caught my special attention. The Navy called for an increase in range by a factor of two over that of the world's best contemporary fighters, and furthermore called for performance superior to that of the Type 96 fighter Model 2-1, which led the world at that time. The new fighter was also supposed to be capable of attaining a speed of 500 km/hr, much faster than the 450 km/hr maximum speed of the Type 96 and superior to any fighter active at that time.

The requirement for two 7.7-mm machine guns and two 20-mm cannons with explosive shells also exceeded the armament provisions of the Type 96, which carried only two 7.7-mm machine guns. Direction-finding equipment had been installed in long-range bombers and reconnaissance aircraft, but this would be the first time in aviation history it was installed in a single-seat fighter. Such a requirement suggested the extremely long range desired for this fighter.

It is not difficult to design an aircraft that is superior in range or performance by sacrificing everything else. But these specifications required the aircraft's range and battle performance to significantly exceed the world's best at the same time that all other performance items equaled the levels of the world's best fighters, including foreign

.ters in prototype design stages. These demands were like asking a decathlon champion to break the 5,000 meter record by a large margin while remaining the best in fencing and being close to the best in other fields. I wondered if it would be possible to fulfill all of the requirements.

Extremely long range and 20-mm cannons are not compatible with good dogfight performance. For good dogfight performance, the aircraft must fly easily and lightly; this means its weight must be low. But in order to have long range, it must carry a great deal of fuel, which in turn would require extra weight for a more extensive fuel system. The addition of the 20-mm cannons certainly would add more weight. This was a downright dilemma.

In my ten years of airplane design, I had seen many fighters that could meet one of their design requirements but failed to meet others. A fighter performs maneuvers which are of a different order of magnitude than those of other types of aircraft. Because of these extreme maneuvers, centrifugal force increases the weight of the aircraft, and under the most severe conditions, the apparent weight can increase by a factor of seven.[3] An aircraft requires a great deal of power simply to fly straight. It is important that weight be held to a minimum so as to allow the fighter to perform high speed flight, sudden climbs, and sharp turns during dogfights.

Fighters have intrinsic difficulties to begin with, but the specifications for the Prototype 12 compounded these difficulties by including many items that would increase the aircraft's weight. I could almost visualize the atmosphere of the conference in which the requirements were established. These requirements, it seemed, were thrown in randomly by the people on the requesting side. Those who developed the specifications were specialists in their respective fields, and they must have done what they thought was necessary in light of Japan's situation at the time.

In particular, the requirement for long range, which was not in the May draft, must have been due to lessons learned in China that year. There had been an incident when proud new Navy bombers went

3. Translators' note: There are many other design conditions that also develop high G levels in which centrifugal force plays no part.

into action without fighter escort at the mid-China front and were downed one after the other by enemy interceptors. After that, Type 96 fighters went along with our bombers and exhibited the power which the Navy specialists expected of them. This proved that the establishment of air superiority using fighters was the key to winning air battles. The Prototype 12 requirements must have been established with particular objectives in mind: 20-mm cannons to destroy large aircraft, range to fly to and from enemy bases, and the ability to fight the enemy aircraft which would be waiting there. As I read the document, I imagined I could hear the requests of Japan, which had been driven into a tight corner. "This is a very difficult task," I said to myself. I lapsed into deep thought as I continued to stare at the requirements while the autumn day dissolved into darkness.

The "Prototype 12 Carrier-Based Fighter" was none other than the name given to the prototype of the Zero fighter, which later was regarded as the King of the Sky during the Pacific war.

CAN SUCH AN AIRPLANE BE DESIGNED?

From that day on, my mind was preoccupied with planning for the Prototype 12 fighter. From the rooftop of the building where our offices were located, we could view the Suzuka Mountains in the west and Ise Bay in the southwest. During good weather, the rooftop was a suitable spot to practice golf swings, but we no longer had time for that. It became a place for our exhausted minds to relax from the task of developing different plans for the new fighter.

The situation for those of us in charge of the design was truly merciless in those days. First, the development of large power plants was slow in Japan. A fighter with the performance requirements of the Prototype 12—especially the incomparable range and the 20-mm cannons mounted for the first time on a carrier-based fighter—could not help but become a large, heavy airplane. For it to have high speed and superior dogfight performance, a light and powerful engine would be needed. Since such a power plant was not available, to my regret, in Japan at that time, it was necessary to design the airplane so light that it defied common sense. Second, the design also had to conserve material, for Japan was nearly resourceless. However, we did have more manpower than any single European nation and about one third that of the United States. Therefore, when we weighed manpower versus material, we were obliged to select a design that emphasized the conservation of material. The United States and Germany, on the other hand, selected manufacturing methods that used more material but saved manpower. Even if they appeared to be rustic, Japan's construction methods necessarily consisted of many assemblies of small parts. In this respect, England, being different from the United States and Germany, followed the same path as Japan. Third, in those days airplanes were selected on the basis of competitive prototypes. This was a system in which the military provided contracts to two or more manufacturers to build a prototype, and selected the best one. But there was a catch to this system, namely, whether the military pilots personally liked the airplane. No matter how well we designed and built it, if the pilot who flew the airplane did not accept it, it would not win the competition. The designer must, therefore, bear in mind the pilot's personal taste. Honestly speaking, I was depressed when I considered these matters. Could we really build such an airplane under these conditions? As I headed home in the dark, cold night, uncertainty filled my mind.

If there was anything which gave me comfort, it was my previous experiences. As a school age child, I had a longing for airplanes. After completing a course of study in aeronautical engineering at the university and starting work, my everyday life was filled with nothing but airplanes. Prior to the Prototype 12, I had designed two other Navy fighters, the Prototype 7 and Prototype 9. These were both very difficult tasks for an inexperienced aeronautical engineer, but somehow I had managed to come through. The Prototype 9 fighter was especially successful; it was later introduced by the Navy as the Type 96 carrier-based fighter and, through its high rating both nationally and internationally, helped to raise the low level of Japanese aircraft closer to that of other nations.

I could not help thinking back to the rough road I had traveled as I now faced yet another challenge: the design of the Prototype 12.

The Search for
a New Fighter

A Dream Staked on Airplanes

I was born in the country near the city of Fujioka, Gunma Prefecture, in 1903, thirty-four years before the time I would receive the planning request for the Prototype 12 fighter. This was, by chance, the same year the Wright brothers made their maiden flight in the United States.

I was a grade school student when World War I began and aircraft first served in combat; it was absorbing to read the newspaper articles describing the European conflict, especially those concerning air battles on the western front. The children's magazines such as *Hikoshonen* and *Bukyosekai* were filled with such stories. In particular, the names of famous airplanes—Nieuport, Spad, Fokker, and Sopwith, as well as other new European fighters—excited my young blood. In my sleep I would often dream of flying in a small airplane of my own construction, high over fields and rivers or sometimes close to the ground.

My interest in airplanes started to fade when I went from junior to senior high school but revived again when I was faced with the decision of what course of study to pursue at the university. There my desire to study aeronautical engineering, particularly in airframes, solidified, especially after talking with a friend of my brother's who was an assistant professor in the newly formed Department of Aeronautics at the University of Tokyo. I began my studies in April 1923.

At that time, the Aeronautics Department was like a small family with only twenty-six students and thirteen instructors, including visiting instructors and professors.

The following month I made my first flight. It was a custom, at that time, for the university to ask the Army or Navy to provide the opportunity for students to be passengers in their airplanes. Those of us who knew of this tradition were anxiously hoping the time would soon come for our flight. Our wish was granted sooner than expected, since one of our fellow students was a Navy lieutenant attending school at the request of his superiors. He took us for a tour of Kasumigaura Naval Base in Chiba Prefecture.

As soon as we arrived at the base, we were taken to a hangar where we saw many kinds of airplanes. They were all biplanes braced by struts and wires which stretched in every direction. One of these, an Avro trainer imported from England, was rolled from the hangar and prepared for flight. As I was at last getting ready to fly, my heart throbbed with excitement. A parachute was strapped on my back; I put on my flight cap and goggles and climbed into the cockpit, squeezing down in the narrow seat and fastening the seat belt. The engine was started and the airplane began to roll. As I looked down, I saw the ground streaming back in a striped pattern. When the bumpy feeling of the ground roll ceased, I knew the wheels were off the ground. I tried to look below but was met by a strong blast of wind in my face. As we climbed higher, the land below began to look like a miniature garden. At an even higher altitude, it was like a colorful map.

Suddenly the horizon in front of me seemed to move to the right and started to roll under the airplane's nose. At the same time, my head was pushed down and I found it took an unusual effort to straighten my neck and raise my hands. This was caused by the acrobatic maneuvering of the airplane, but at the time, I had no idea what was happening. After remaining this way for a while, the ground rotated in the opposite direction and the airplane returned to normal; at the same time, the unusual forces acting on my body faded away.

Next, the horizon in front of me began to sink. As before, my head and hands became extraordinarily heavy and the horizon completely disappeared. Immediately, the other horizon appeared from above and behind me and the ground hung over my head. I felt as if I were being pulled by the base of my neck and an awful sensation ran through my stomach. The ground continued to rotate and the horizon sank below me. While my head and hands became heavy again, the horizon and the ground that had been in front of me in the beginning came down from above me, and finally the airplane returned to its normal flight attitude. The airplane continued its flight for a while without doing anything unusual. But before I had time to relax, my body was pushed to one side, and suddenly I saw the ground approaching from the front and spinning in a diagonal direction. I started to feel nauseated as a result of being thrown about so much. I do not know how many times we turned but finally the ground stopped rotating. Again my head and hands were pushed down, and my perspective returned to normal as the horizon came down from above in front of me. This ended the acrobatic stunts and the aircraft landed. I was later to learn the first maneuver was a left vertical turn, the second was a loop, and the third was a spin. Since the maneuvers took place without any explanation or warning, I had no idea which way the airplane actually moved. As I stood on the ground, I was still dizzy.

The airplane, which moves in three dimensions, is much faster and more complicated than any land vehicle. The forces produced by its acceleration greatly affect the passengers. The pilot who maneuvers the machine must be able to move his hands and feet freely, thus causing the airplane to respond. During maneuvers, his body will feel unusual forces acting on it and he will see strange sights outside of the cockpit. It takes a great deal of difficult training for a pilot to develop his skills. Accumulated flight training will enable him to sense the attitude of his airplane relative to the ground and the type of motion his airplane is performing, as long as he can see the ground and the horizon. I soon realized it was the designer's duty to produce an easily controllable airplane so as to reduce the pilot's burden as much as possible. This experience further stirred my dreams of airplane design.

I really enjoyed the next three years of college. Because aeronautical science and technology had only been in existence for a short period of time and had not been systematized even in the Western nations where the airplane was born, our lectures were unsystematic and the atmosphere was very relaxed. Students and instructors shared an intimate classroom atmosphere and this resulted in free expression and fresh ideas, which were important during this pioneering period. I studied hard, as I felt the demand of the times for aeronautical technology would someday rest on my shoulders. After three years of college, I joined Mitsubishi Internal Combustion Engine Company Limited, which later became Mitsubishi Heavy Industries, Nagoya Aircraft Manufacturing Plant. I was to be a member of the airframe design section.

I JOIN MITSUBISHI

When I started my engineering career, the Nagoya Aircraft Manufacturing Plant and the Nakajima Aircraft Company of Ohta-Cho, Gunma Prefecture, were the two largest military aircraft manufacturers in Japan. The building which housed the design group was a long flat stucco structure, and when I walked down the halls, wearing the new shoes my elder brother had given me as a gift for joining Mitsubishi, the floors would squeak. On the east side of the building was a large vacant lot which was sprouting a fresh crop of weeds. During the lunch hour, some people would practice golf swings there and occasionally the company training plane would take off and land.

With my heart swelling with hope on the first day, I entered the room where the design section was located. All together, there were about fifty people there. The desks were each equipped with a drawing board and were neatly arranged on either side of the aisle down the middle. The room was full of action; some people were engaged in design work, while others were talking or referring to drawings.

There was no formal welcoming and I was told to report anytime during April. It seemed to be quite a carefree atmosphere. When I was told where my immediate supervisor was located, I walked over to see him. I found a large man with a dark complexion who suddenly

Sapporo

SEA OF JAPAN

Nagano

Kagamigahara

Gifu

Kyoto

Kobe

Hiroshima

Gunma

Karuizawa

Kasumigaura

Tokyo

Yokosuka

Nagoya

Osaka

Nagasaki

PACIFIC OCEAN

0   100 km

stood up and greeted me, saying, "I am Hattori." This was Mr. Jyoji Hattori, who would lead the airframe design section of Mitsubishi for many years to come. Mr. Hattori, who was chief of the design section at that time, took me to one of the groups and introduced me, saying, "I want him to spend time here with you." This group was designing an Army fighter under the supervision of Professor Bowman from Germany. The Japanese chief of the group was Mr. Nakata, who was next in line to Mr. Hattori in the chain of command; he was waiting for my arrival.

Everyone was friendly to me, and I was given a desk near the window so I would have good light. This was a bit of a problem, however, since during the summer months the desk was continuously covered with fine dust carried into the room by the ocean breeze. I would sweep the dust off of my desk using the brush which engineers usually use to sweep eraser particles from their drawings.

In the design section were draftsmen, who prepared drawings; engineering aides, who assisted engineers; and also design engineers, who were the senior members of the group. In the next room there were many young girls called tracers, who made tracings of simple drawings. Engineering aides occasionally became acquainted with them and some were later married. Sometimes I used to remark, while having a cup of coffee with my senior engineer or other coworkers, "Did you see that cute tracer?"

These were the first steps I took toward becoming a design engineer. I worked hard during the day, and after arriving home, I would read aviation magazines from America, England, and Germany. Our professors had warned us upon graduation, "Don't forget to keep studying." Despite my good intentions, however, I usually could not read more than five lines of German without getting sleepy.

My First Design

A specialized aircraft industry, modeled after those of the advanced nations, was just being developed in Japan in the late 1920s. Already the tradition had been established whereby the Army or Navy granted contracts to companies for prototype designs and eventually selected one company's aircraft for production. The Navy Armament Reduction Conferences, which were held in Washington and London after World War I, had resulted in severe limitations on the number of Japanese military ships. However, it was necessary to expand our military forces, since the international situation did not allow us to relax. As a result of this, all eyes focused on air power. But Japanese air strength was far behind the times and the Navy was keenly aware of this. The Navy decided to implement a policy that would make Japan independent of other nations in regard to aviation technology; it was called "Project Aviation Technology Independence."

The new policy was developed during the period from 1931 to 1932 and resulted in the design and construction of many indigenous aircraft. It also established the Naval Aeronautical Establishment as a central organization to coordinate the efforts of the many small aeronautical laboratories which were scattered throughout the country. In 1932, the first five Prototype 7 aircraft were ordered. My first assignment as a chief designer was for one of these prototypes, the Prototype 7 carrier-based fighter.

THE BIRTH OF JAPAN'S NEWEST FIGHTERS

It had been five years since I joined Mitsubishi. During this time I designed various aircraft components, calculated performance, and determined strength characteristics. I had been sent to Germany, England, France, and America to visit their airplane factories, study their publications, and talk to their designers. Based on these experiences, I knew it would not take Japan very long to catch up with their small-airplane technology if we had proper government priorities and policy. However, it could not be done in a single leap. This was about the extent of my background and experience up to this time.

LEARNING FROM MISTAKES

To be a chief designer was a very great responsibility, yet I could not be daunted by this forever. At first I wondered why the company would appoint such an immature person as myself to be the chief designer of a new fighter. Perhaps my superiors felt my lack of experience would be an advantage, since I would not be bound by tradition. But how would it look if I allowed the Japanese aircraft industry to remain behind the world indefinitely? I considered this and decided to tackle the job head on.

Because this was my first time in charge of a new airplane's design, I had trouble deciding upon the basic configuration. I wanted to try a cantilevered monoplane, which was a new single-wing type without external supports. But there were no data in Japan relevant to such a design, since none had been built here before. On the other hand, there were plenty of reference data which covered biplanes, since they were the standard fighters in the world's military forces in those days. At the outset, everything would be easy if a biplane configuration were attempted. But later on, in the design of the final prototype, we would have to deal with a host of complications if we were to win the keen competition. In addition, many foreign nations were reportedly investigating the monoplane; I could not be sure they would not be successful. As I pondered the decision, Lt. Comdr. Jiro Saha, who was in charge of fighter design at aeronautics headquarters, said, "It's okay, go ahead and do it." I was very thankful for his encouragement, which helped me make up my mind.

That was how I selected the configuration for the world's first monoplane carrier-based fighter. I used a new style of metal skin construction known as semi-monocoque in the fuselage, but unfortunately I could not use a metal wing and had to settle for a fabric-covered unit, since our manufacturing technicians did not believe they could satisfactorily rivet metal skin to a small wing. For the wing main spar, I used a new style which had been under study by the Navy and later would be used on both the Prototype 9 and Prototype 12 fighters.

Supervising the overall project kept me so busy that I was unable to provide much leadership at the detail design stage. I was a chief designer with plenty of spirit but few results. Although to meet the deadline we had to move forward with our work, I was unsatisfied with many things.

Biplane
This was the most common
type of fighter up to the early
1930s. It had a tight turning
radius but limited top speed.

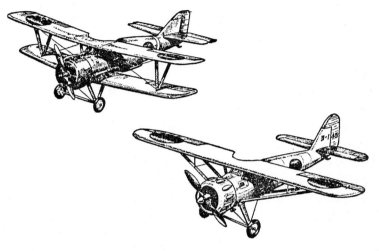

Parasol
In comparison to the biplane,
this type had greater speed
but a larger turning radius.

Low-Wing Monoplane
This was the most advanced
type, but there were many
technical problems. Nevertheless, I decided to use this
style.

As the drawings materialized into many parts, many faults became noticeable. Previously, I had not paid attention to small details, but now they began to bother me. My biggest complaint was the aircraft's overall appearance; with its thick wing, raised cockpit for better visibility, round vertical tail, and fixed landing gear, which resembled a wide pair of trousers, the airplane looked like a slow-witted duck. My next objection was that there were too many protrusions on the aircraft's surface. These irregularities would be a major source of drag during high speed flight. Also, the equipment and accessories were poorly located, and there were many complaints concerning the weight and appearance of the frame fasteners.

But, somehow, in March 1933 we completed the first model of the Prototype 7 fighter, knowing that despite its many faults we had done our best. Its stability and control characteristics during ordinary flight were not bad, but as a fighter it had many problems. During the last portion of company flight tests conducted at Kagamigahara airfield at Gifu, the upper half of the vertical tail broke away suddenly while the plane was in a dive at about 2,000 meters altitude. The pilot confirmed the damage and bailed out after cutting the engine. The then pilotless airplane pulled up by itself, wandered to the left and right, and disappeared over a hill. We found the wreckage on the bank of the Kiso River about a kilometer away. When it crashed, it must have tumbled over rocks. The second model of the Prototype 7 was delivered to the Navy and it also crashed during flight testing by the Yokosuka Air Corps. It suddenly went into an unrecoverable spin.

Our competitor, Nakajima, submitted a familiar high-wing or parasol type of monoplane with strut-braced wings. But the Navy disqualified this machine also. Out of five Prototype 7 airplanes tested, the only model that passed was a refined fabric-covered scout seaplane, a biplane.

Despite my enthusiasm, our Prototype 7 failed to perform well, and its life ended tragically. But I learned a great deal from its design and testing. Looking back, I think we made the proper decision when we decided to try to build this low-wing monoplane, and I owe a great deal to the generous attitude of the higher management of my company, and to the Navy people we worked with during its development, for their encouragement. By designing this aircraft, I was able to grasp the future role of single-engine fighter aircraft faster than anyone else in Japan. I think I also learned the knack of bringing out the best in my subordinates; or perhaps I should say, I matured.

MY AIMS FOR THE PROTOTYPE 9

The opportunity soon arrived to make use of what we had learned from the Prototype 7. In February 1934 the Navy ordered a new carrier-based fighter as well as three other types of aircraft for their Prototype 9 competition. Once again, Mitsubishi and Nakajima were to compete for the carrier-based fighter. This time, the Naval Aeronautics Headquarters, after consulting with fleet staff headquarters, eased some of the design requirements.

One of the features usually expected of a Navy fighter was the ability to land on the deck of a carrier. For this competition, however, this requirement was eliminated and the range specification was also eased. The airplane was simply to be a single-seat fighter. I again was given the job of chief designer for the Prototype 9 fighter. This time I felt differently than I had when we started out on the Prototype 7, since I had now experienced the complete design process and was better able to communicate with my staff. On top of this, we had much more freedom to use our own ingenuity to meet the aircraft's performance requirements.

I immediately called together the chief members of the design team, and we discussed the state of world aviation and Japan's position among other nations. I also explained my concrete plans and ideas. All personnel exchanged opinions and appeared to be pleased; our laughter was endless.

In those days, fabric-covered biplanes were the master fighters of carrier-based air fleets. For land-based fighters, however, this was not the case, since all-metal types had been introduced one after the other. An example was the low-wing metal monoplane introduced by Dewoitine of France. Having seen this trend develop, I organized the

Prototype 9 concept in detail from the start. The basic configuration was similar to the Prototype 7—that is, it was to be a low-wing monoplane with a fixed gear. Apart from this, everything else was different. This time, the airplane was all metal, including the wing, and many progressive details were added, such as the use of flush rivets everywhere on the exterior surface. Flush rivets leave no protruding heads on the surface after the riveting is complete, whereas rivets that are not flush will leave a head, thereby causing air resistance, or drag. By using the flush fasteners we were able to decrease drag by a large margin and increase the aircraft's speed. By using a metal skin I was able to decrease the wing's thickness and could more easily maintain the proper surface shape to further reduce drag.

I made the fuselage as slim as possible. For the power plant, I used a single-row radial type which was different from the one on the Prototype 7, and it provided more visibility because the pilot could look between the cylinders during landing. This eliminated the necessity of having his seat and the machine guns located in a raised position; the new airplane would appear more stylish.

The selection of the engine is so important that it frequently decides the fate of the aircraft. The engine used on the Prototype 7 was a product of Mitsubishi, but it had many problems, such as oil leaks and being heavy for its power output. From the viewpoint of power, weight, and size, the 550 hp Nakajima Kotobuki Type 5 engine used on the Nakajima Prototype 7 fighter was the most suitable power plant for our Prototype 9, which was to be significantly lighter than our Prototype 7. I felt bad for the engine division of Mitsubishi, since I preferred to use the competitor's engine. But Mitsubishi wanted to win the Navy contract and this made me determined to use the Kotobuki Type 5. The company and the Navy readily consented.

After the engine decision was made, one of the team members came to me and said, "This means, for the Prototype 9, Nakajima will probably use the same engine; therefore, airframe design becomes more important." I wholeheartedly agreed with him and was even more aware of my responsibility, which, in turn, added to the excitement of the contest.

The most important task after power plant selection was to determine how much we could reduce airframe weight. Because Japan was just then becoming an industrial nation, we were behind America and the strong nations of Europe in the race to develop high horsepower engines. In a nutshell, it was the Japanese aircraft designer's task to compensate for power deficiency by reducing airframe weight.

About that time in America, the use of retractable landing gear was gaining popularity on small single-engine aircraft, and this idea was also catching on among fighter designers. But this style of landing gear increased weight and complicated manufacturing, as well as increasing cost because of the additional retracting mechanism. The Navy had requested that the fighter be very maneuverable. To this end, the fighter must be light. Since this was the reason for selecting the lightweight engine, I could not justify the additional weight of a retractable landing gear. Instead I used a slender fixed-position landing gear with streamlined fairings. I expected to obtain about the same drag reduction as would have been realized by a retractable gear, since I was using flush rivets all over the airframe. In the final analysis, the reason for not adopting the retractable gear was not a simple rationalization to cover up the disadvantage of using a low-power engine, but was instead a positive attitude which emphasized weight control.

The work progressed at a rapid rate and everything went quite smoothly with this novel fighter. Each day I was very busy; every night I came home late but felt no discomfort.

The Birth of the Type 96 Fighter, the Predecessor of the Prototype 12 Fighter

The Prototype 9 fighter, the direct predecessor of the Prototype 12 fighter, was completed in January 1935. The airframe weight, which we had thought of as our biggest problem, ended up being less than the original estimate. However, the skin had a quilted appearance caused by the unskillful installation of the flush rivets. These dimples were especially noticeable in contrast to the rest of the shiny duralumin suface. We solved the problem by filling the depressions with putty and painting the airframe with a thick coat of Navy specification ash green paint. Then the airframe was polished.

Although our competitor also designed a low-wing monoplane, it had fabric wing surfaces with bracing wires on both upper and lower surfaces. This was an old style which had been popular in America about three years earlier. As a result, when we learned that the weight of our airframe was within the original estimate, we knew the game was almost over. Our competitor had started flight testing prior to us and we learned that the maximum speed of its airplane was slightly greater than 400 km/hr. We began flight tests at Kagamigahara field and soon found our fighter had good stability and control characteristics in addition to a maximum speed in excess of 440 km/hr.

The Navy then officially recognized the maximum speed of our aircraft under normal weight conditions to be 450km/hr at an altitude of 3,200 meters based on naval flight tests. The maximum speeds of other Japanese fighters of those days were 290 km/hr for the Navy Type 90, and 320 km/hr for the Army Type 92; their replacements had speeds of 350 km/hr for the Navy Type 95, and 380 km/hr for the experimental Army Ki—10, which was later known as the Army Type 95. As can be seen from these figures, the maximum speeds of fighters increased at the rate of approximately 20 km/hr per year. On top of this, since the Type 95 had an 820 hp engine and the Ki—10 had an engine of 950 hp, it was natural for the Prototype 9 single-seat fighter with only a 550 hp engine to create a sensation in the Japanese aviation community when it established a high speed record approximately 100 km/hr better than any other fighter.

During this time, I vividly remember how Lt. Comdr. Yoshito Kobayashi, of the Aeronautical Establishment, repeated the dangerous high speed tests many times, with the pilots flying at maximum speeds at an altitude of only about thirty meters over the temporary Kagamigahara test course. He was the most dedicated man I knew in the Aeronautical Establishment engaged in the development of Navy fighters.

At first, the Navy decided our original calculated maximum speed of 410 km/hr was too optimistic and decided 400 km/hr would be more realistic. During flight tests, however, it soon became clear that a speed of over 430 km/hr could be easily obtained. This made the Navy officers happy but put them in an awkward position, since they had not believed such a high speed was possible. The Navy's chief inspector in the Nagoya district, who was in charge of coordination between our company and the Aeronautical Establishment, was especially pleased with the results, and he took delight in needling the representatives from the Aeronautical Establishment by saying, "Don't ever mention words such as inspection and leadership."

The next task was to determine if the Prototype 9 was a good dogfighter, a quality desired by the Navy more than anything else. The Prototype 9 certainly had exceptionally high maximum speed and rate of climb. But a fighter would further require good turning performance, sensitive control response, and stability so as to serve as a good gun platform. Monoplanes had long been considered inferior to biplanes in terms of turning radius, and this was one reason why most of the world's fighter designers would not give up biplanes.

In those days, the Navy's Yokosuka Naval Air Corps was in charge of tests to determine combat characteristics. The group that handled fighters was their own fighter squadron, and during 1934–35 it was nicknamed the "Genda Circus," as it was composed of Japan's best pilots and was commanded by Lt. Minoru Genda. The fate of our Prototype 9 single seater depended entirely upon the critical eyes of these pilots. Their duties were to determine the aircraft's flying qualities, correct any weak points, and learn how best to handle or use the new machine. They also had an equally important duty: to determine future Navy fighter requirements for the defense of Japan.

Under these circumstances, a mock air battle was carried out in the fall of 1935. The opponents were the Navy's latest biplane Type 95 fighters, British Hawker Nimrods, French Dewaitine D 510s, German Heinkel He 112s, and American Seversky 2PAs. It was thrilling to look up at the mock fighting of these airplanes with their silver wings sparkling in the blue sky. Our Prototype 9 was able to win easily over all fighters except the Type 95 biplane and we discovered that the Prototype 9 could win over the Type 95 if climbs and dives were allowed in the tactics. This discovery was to have profound influence in developing battle tactics for fighters with high speeds and high

rates of climb. It also answered the question of whether the Prototype 9 was a good dogfighter.

Thus, an unbelievable fighter was born, with a top speed equal to
the world's best and a fighting ability superior to all other aircraft.
It was the first of a unique series of Japanese fighters. Like a Judo
wrestler who is a master of both the "standing throw" and "on the
mat" techniques, these aircraft were extremely adaptable. In the
fall of 1936, the Prototype 9 was officially accepted as the Type 96,
No. 1 Carrier-Based Fighter.

The birth of the Type 96 helped to build confidence among Japanese aircraft designers, who prior to that time felt self-conscious and
doubtful of their abilities. The Type 96 fighter played a significant
role in determining the shape of single-engine fighters for years thereafter, and certainly it contributed to the accelerated development of
Japanese technology. Army and Navy squadrons soon equipped
themselves with the Type 96 monoplane and the improved Type 97
model in an effort to catch up with the rest of the world.

THE FIRST VICTORY FOR THE TYPE 96

The ability of the Type 96 fighter was soon shown in the Second
Sino-Japanese War, which began to really heat up in July 1937. It
was the morning of 19 September when I first learned about it. My
working hours started at 7:30 A.M., and I would often read the newspaper as I ate breakfast. On that day I opened the paper and found
an article with a large picture stating that the Type 96 fighter had
downed some thirty enemy aircraft over Nanking. I unintentionally
gasped aloud. Normally, at home, I never talked about my work,
but this was an exception and I showed the papers to the rest of
my family. When I reached the office, with the paper in my hand,
everybody was talking about the article. According to the battle
records, twelve Type 96 fighters took off from a Shanghai suburb on
18 September escorting Type 96 bombers and Type 95 seaplane reconnaissance aircraft on a mission to bomb Nanking, the capital of
China. The Type 96 fighters destroyed thirty-three enemy fighters

in only fifteen minutes over the sky of Nanking. Following this first victory, Type 96 fighters went on to down many enemy planes, including American, English, and Russian designs. On 2 December, they downed about ten Russian I–16 fighters over Nanking, and that was the last time Chinese planes were seen in the Nanking skies.

Following the Nanking air raid, Navy fighters advanced deeply into inland China, a mission completely different from the one for which they were designed—guarding the sky over military ships. Until this time, it had been considered best to employ attack bombers against enemy bases so as to destroy planes on the ground. But the Sino-Japanese air battles taught us clearly it was more effective to down enemy airplanes in the sky with their pilots in them. The Japanese Navy decided to introduce, before any other country, the concept of using fighters to obtain air superiority. This tactic would later be carried out on a large scale by our fighters in the Pacific during World War II. Similar tactics were not used in the European theater until the last stages of the war. Hence there were no dogfighting aircraft in Europe similar to ours.[1]

The success of the Type 96 was certainly a big surprise at the time, but the rate of progress in fighter design has always been very rapid. Even the best fighters become obsolete within two years during times of war and four years during times of peace, and the Type 96 would not be an exception to this rule. A new fighter, which could be used efficiently during the coming air war, was needed. Thus, the concept of the Prototype 12 was formed and with it came the requirements for almost unbelievable performance capabilities.

---

1. Translators' note: Many nations experimented with extremely maneuverable fighters prior to the beginning of World War II in Europe, but rejected the tactical concept of dogfighting adopted by Japan.

The Challenge of Impossibilities

To Make the Impossible Possible

When I received the request for planning for the Prototype 12, news of the Type 96 fighter's activities was reported in the papers almost daily. Certainly, the reason why the Type 96 was the best fighter of those times was because it utilized the most current design technology. Having worked close to my limits when designing the Type 96, I could see how severe the Prototype 12 requirements were. Later, I was to think many times about what constituted good fighter characteristics.

Up to that time, we had successfully completed the design of two new airplanes, both of which had appeared very difficult to develop at the beginning of the projects. I had been successful in my campaign to develop these aircraft independent of foreign technology, even though it had always been customary for Japanese airplane designers to lag a few years behind the advanced nations. I thought perhaps it was possible for us to create a completely new fighter which would lead the world if I really put my head to work and used my brain. By such thoughts, I encouraged myself.

Because of overwork, I neglected my health and became ill. This forced me to be absent from work for some time during the important period after the planning request was received. Luckily, I recovered without becoming seriously ill, but I realized the importance of being healthy, and my superior gave me some strong but good advice: to take care of my health and get on with the project.

Soon after that, the real design period of the Prototype 12 fighter began. At that time, we were engaged in many small modification jobs on the Type 96 fighter as a result of operational experience gained during the Second Sino-Japanese War. In addition to our efforts to create the Prototype 12, we still had to take care of its predecessor, the Type 96. I am thankful, even today, to all the members of the design team, who fully cooperated with each other as well as with their not so healthy leader.

In order to tackle this difficult project, I suspected that we would have to break away from established traditions and what often is referred to as common sense. Although for a designer this was an unconventional way to think, I believed it was necessary to shed new light on our design practices and specifications. Nothing should be accepted blindly, regardless of how traditional it might be. When we worked on the Type 96, we were able to give it a shape completely different from earlier fighters. Was there not something we could do this time in some esoteric area which had not yet been fully explored?

I started to work on the engine selection and made a preliminary weight estimate. Of all types of airplanes, none are so dependent upon engine selection as are fighters. Only when the engine has been selected can a designer produce a draft of the airframe. In the case of the Prototype 12, as previously stated, the Mitsubishi Kinsei Type 46 and the Zuisei Type 13 were listed as candidate engines, the Kinsei being the more powerful of the two. If we used the Kinsei, we could have an airplane with high performance and high speed in one jump. For just that reason I felt it should be selected. This was in keeping with my philosophy that it would be better to design a high performance fighter in one big leap rather than to eventually reach that goal by making numerous small improvements to a lower performance aircraft over the span of its lifetime.

But there was a fateful obstacle in using the Kinsei: it required a bigger airframe. The Kinsei was more powerful than the Zuisei, and it also was larger, heavier, and consumed more fuel. Because of this, the airframe would be larger than if a smaller engine were used, and the fuel weight would be greater. In order to carry the increased weight, the wing must be larger and the fuselage and tail would also have to be larger. This, in turn, would require a stronger landing gear and yet another increase in airframe size.

A quick weight estimate showed the airplane's weight would be about 3,000 kg. This was acceptable for a land-based plane, but pilots accustomed to flying small 1,600-kg Type 96 fighters would not readily accept the heavy new fighter. And this would mean the loss of the Prototype 12 contract. In contrast, if we used the Zuisei engine, the airplane's weight was estimated to be about 2,300 kg; the wing span would be in the neighborhood of twelve meters with a wing area compatible with good fighter performance. I thought this was about the maximum weight that the pilots would accept. Instead of pondering the future of the aircraft, our immediate job was to win the contract. I decided, "Okay, let's get on with it." When I reported my decision to use the Zuisei to Mr. Hattori, he approved.

STREAMLINES AND STRENGTH

Once the engine had been selected, the next task was to sketch the airframe with the engine mounted. There were many problems yet to be solved, but at this time I had in my mind a rough sketch of the airframe. It would appear as a more refined Type 96 with trim surfaces and lines. I drew up a rough three-view sketch on a piece of paper in front of me.

First came the side view. I drew the fuselage lines to match the engine cowl, which was already fixed when the engine selection was made. The sizes of the vertical tail and pilot's compartment were approximated based on experience. A fuel tank was placed between the engine and cockpit, and after approximating the fuselage's center of gravity, I drew in the wing. Then I roughly selected the landing gear length, using the diameter of the propeller as a controlling factor, and finally, keeping front and rear visibility and low drag in mind, I sketched in the canopy.

Next came the plan view. The aerodynamically clean look from the side view was used to determine the planform of the fuselage. One problem to resolve was the shape of the wing planform. I was already thinking of an advanced style instead of what was used on the Type 96. In those days, a near elliptic shape for monoplane wing planforms was prevalent, as in the Type 96, but for the Prototype 12 I was determined to use a straight taper with a narrow tip. The lines of the new aircraft began to take shape as I configured the wing and drew in a matching horizontal tail.

Next, I approximated the internal storage requirements in the wing, since I planned to use a retractable landing gear. This storage area was shown by means of dotted lines. Just outboard of the landing gear, space was provided for the 20-mm cannons, which were very powerful armament for those days. I also had an idea for the size and location of the wing fuel tanks. Last came the front view. With this, the initial stage of my job was completed. The new airplane appeared to have both speed and power suitable for what would become the world's latest and strongest fighter.

After that, a detailed three-view drawing would be made based on more precise calculations. Most of our time was spent determining the dimensions and shape of the wing. First we would have to draw in and determine the details of the retractable landing gear and the 20-mm cannons. Then we could turn to the question of the wing planform and thickness. I asked Messrs. Kato, Sone, and Hatakenaka, who were the chief members of my design team, to come to my desk. Mr. Kato was responsible for designing landing gears for Navy aircraft; Mr. Sone had mastered the art of structural design while he was in charge of stress calculations for the Type 96; Mr. Hatakenaka was a veteran of armament installation. They were all excellent design engineers and were my right-hand men. It was not necessary to say a great deal to them, since we understood each other implicitly. "To begin with, I would like to start from here," I said and showed them my three-view drawing. I asked Mr. Kato to work on the landing gear attachment and retraction mechanism, Mr. Hatakenaka to design the details for mounting the cannons, and Mr. Sone to come up with an idea of wing dimensions and structure to house the gear and armament. Some time later, the wing shape and thickness would be decided by our joint efforts.

As work progressed, we made drawings of a smooth fuselage which blended properly with the engine and cockpit. Drawings were also made of the tail surfaces so that they would match the entire package. I repeated in greater detail my estimation of the weight and center of gravity. In this manner, the Prototype 12 fighter was created.

The signs of winter were creeping upon the outside world, but we did not notice them. Still thinking that the fields were full of green grass, I was surprised one day, as I sat in the cafeteria, to see the outside green had turned to yellow while I was single-mindedly chasing ideas for the Prototype 12.

Labor Pains Begin

The contours of the Prototype 12 were decided by the engineers, other members of the design team, and myself, but we soon faced a more difficult task. Our utmost efforts would be required to incorporate in our configuration the various performance specifications demanded by the Navy. The more I thought about the methods necessary to satisfy the Navy's request, the more obvious its severity became. I groaned daily at my desk. During the lunchtime break, talk would usually consist of gossip about the habits of Navy pilots, but occasionally the performance specification items lingered in my mind. "It would make the thing much easier," I thought, "if they would withdraw just one of their requirements."

Meantime, 1938 had arrived and a joint government-industry meeting on the request for planning of the Prototype 12 fighter was scheduled to be held 17 January, after the holiday season. As usual, the meeting took place in the conference room of the Naval Aeronautical Establishment in Yokosuka. Four of us from Mitsubishi, including Mr. Hattori, reported to the establishment that cold morning with our coat collars turned up to help us keep warm. On the way, we were each engrossed in our own thoughts and only silence accompanied the white clouds of our breath in the cold air.

Representing the Navy were Rear Adm. Misao Wada, chief of the engineering division, Aeronautical Headquarters, and Vice Adm. Koichi Hanajima, director of the Aeronautical Establishment. Other Navy personnel were present, making a total of about twenty. Included among these was Lt. Comd. Minoru Genda, who had been at the Sino-Japanese front lines only a few days earlier and was radiating with the spirit of battle. Industry was represented by five people from Nakajima and the four of us from Mitsubishi.

During the meeting, Admiral Wada and Admiral Hanajima spoke of the future of the war on the Chinese continent as well as the acute international tension which existed at the time. They emphasized the importance of the Prototype 12 fighter. Next, Commander Genda spoke. He vividly described the air battles of the Type 95 and Type 96 fighters from his combat experiences as an aviation staff officer of the Second Joint Air Force. Specifically, he stressed the importance of dogfight performance and range for the new prototype fighter.

Following that, we had a formal discussion concerning the request for planning. The industry representatives tended to remain quiet. The discussions were mostly to confirm the reasons for the severe requirements, and it seemed unlikely that the Navy would withdraw even one of the requirements. But in due time, the chairman sought our opinion by asking, "By the way, what do the designers think?"

I stood up determinedly and, even though I thought my opinion would be rejected, I said, "I think the performance target levels for the new fighter are too high, even considering the state of the art anywhere in the world. Would it be asking too much for one or possibly two items to be withdrawn?" Momentarily the atmosphere in the room was tense. Representatives from industry did not say anything, including Mr. Hattori, but they were silently nodding their heads. The Naval representatives facing us started to whisper among themselves about the unexpected question. But, eventually, their reply was as expected, "No, we can't withdraw anything." Having anticipated their response, I made no further comments. And, in listening to the discussions which followed, I felt we must face our difficult task with renewed determination.

In later days, Commander Genda was to give his impression of the conference. He stated, "Even for an excellent engineer, I believe it must have been very difficult to design an aircraft that would satisfy the impossible, incompatible requirements and achieve such high levels of performance." How true his statement was. The labor pains to deliver the Zero fighter really began at that time.

Formation of the Design Team

As soon as we returned to Nagoya, I and the other design engineers got together with Mr. Hattori and discussed how we should carry out the project from that point. Everybody looked grave. It was clear from the meeting at the Aeronautical Establishment that the Navy would not withdraw even a single performance item from the requirements. Two things must be done immediately. One was to decide upon a firm design policy so that we could transform ideas to a complete design; the other was to organize the design team.

The design team was divided into five groups: computing, structures, propulsion, armament, and landing gear. Most groups consisted of from three to five members, including those who joined us later. The organization was as follows:

Section Chief	Jyoji Hattori
Chief Design Engineer	Jiro Horikoshi
Computing	Yoshitoshi Sone (*Chief*)
	Teruo Tojo, Takeshi Nakamura (later in 1940 Sadao Kobayshi and Masao Kawabe replaced Tojo and Nakamura)
Structures	Yoshitoshi Sone (*Chief*)
	Yoshio Yoshikawa, Sadao Doi, Toshihiko Narahara, Seiichi Mizoguchi, Shigeo Suzumura, Shokichi Tomita, Jyoji Kawamura, Masao Tomoyama
Propulsion	Den-ichiro Inoue (*Chief*)
	Shotaro Tanaka (leadman), Kiichiro Fujiwara, Ken-ichiro Ubuta, Kazuya Yasue, Tadami Yamada

Armament	Yoshimi Hatakenaka (*Chief*)
	Yoichi Ohashi, Hideo Koda, Naoichi Takeda, Mitsuyoshi Eguchi, Shozo Shibayama, Masahiko Morikawa
Landing Gear	Sadahiko Kato (*Chief*)
	Takeyoshi Mori, Keijiro Nakao

There also were many other temporary helpers. The principal members of each group had been on my team since the time we designed the Type 96, and all knew each other. I cannot overemphasize how much this helped in accomplishing the difficult task we faced.

In addition, our leader and chief, Mr. Hattori, provided his young subordinates with mature guidance and encouraged designers to experiment with new concepts and ideas. Mitsubishi Aircraft owes much to this man for making possible the continuous creation of original designs which eventually resulted in our company becoming the national leader during the period when Japan's aviation technology became independent.

ESTABLISHMENT OF THE DESIGN POLICY

The second item of business we had to take care of immediately was the establishment of a design policy. Aviation design work first begins with the conception of an idea in the mind of the chief designer. Next comes a rough weight estimate, based on past designs, and then an estimation of wing area is made. After this is accomplished, performance can be estimated. A rough three-view drawing is then prepared from which the chief designer can explain the concept for critical review by the group chiefs. This review includes a discussion of weight goals and performance estimates.

We had already reached the critical review stage prior to the 17 January conference, and each group was ready to design the main parts for which it was responsible, while at the same time maintaining close coordination with the other groups. At this point, a clear, precise design policy was necessary.

Among his other responsibilities, the chief designer must improve the accuracy of target weights, performance estimates, and dimensions as he continues to refine his concept. As additional information becomes available, he modifies the overall design, quickly transmitting these modifications to the other group chiefs. He also receives reports from each group chief and consults with others, if necessary.

For over two months I kept thinking about the design policy from many different angles. At this stage of the project I sometimes communicated with the group chiefs about details, but usually my job did not permit me to consult anyone else. In a way it was a lonely job.

While at the office, it was easy for me to remain involved with the current work, and since the project was foremost in my mind, I sometimes remained absorbed in it as I rode in the crowded commuter trains or when I was home. At times, I would wake in the middle of the night and think about the new fighter while gazing into the darkness. Sometimes I could not sleep at all, although I went to bed late at night. I was told a nightcap at bedtime would help, but I was born a poor hand at drinking.

Toward the end of 1937, four major design problems had been organized in my mind: (1) the selection of the engine; (2) the selection of the propeller; (3) a weight reduction program; and (4) aerodynamic design, that is, a design that would reduce drag and provide ideal stability and control characteristics at the same time. As far as the engine was concerned, I had already decided to use the Zuisei and this was confirmed at the 17 January conference.

The propeller selection was next. We were to use a new type known as a constant speed unit, which had been specified by the Navy. Propellers previously used on our fighters were fixed pitch units with blades rigidly attached to the hub. They were designed to operate at full rpm and permitted the use of maximum power only while flying at maximum speed. Because of this, when an airplane flew at a speed other than maximum—during a climb or takeoff for example—a greater load was impressed on the propeller, engine power was reduced, and optimum use of the available power could not be realized. This is analogous to a car that has only high gear: when starting from rest or climbing a slope at low speed, it cannot utilize the power of its en-

At low speed

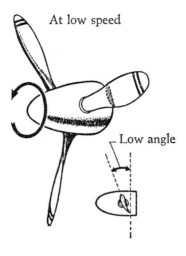

Low angle

At high speed

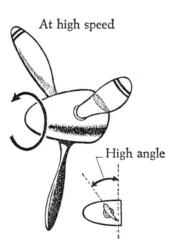

High angle

The propeller was called a constant speed unit and its blade angle automatically changed according to the airplane's speed to allow the engine to develop maximum power at all times. The effectiveness of this unit was demonstrated during dogfights, which required that the aircraft's speed change very quickly from low to high.

gine because of reduced engine rpm. In contrast, the constant speed propeller reduces propeller blade angle at low speeds and increases it at high speeds, thus changing the pitch automatically according to the airplane's speed. Maximum power can be realized from maximum rpm throughout the speed range of the airplane. The speed of a fighter changes an infinite number of times from climb to dive, especially during a dogfight, and if the fighter is very fast, the constant speed propeller becomes even more effective, since the airplane it drives has a wide range of speed. The decision to specify this type of propeller for the Prototype 12 was understandable, and the Navy also pressured industry to import engineering know-how from the United States. The engine and propeller development and modification programs were beyond our control and we airframe designers were helpless to assist in the solution of those problems regardless of how much we worried about them.

The Biggest Problem—Weight Reduction

The biggest problem we faced was weight reduction. Significant weight reduction could not be achieved by using ordinary methods of design. Everybody had to make positive efforts to reduce weight at all times. We followed what might be called a basic weight control approach. This was something we thought about during the engine selection period; it was the concept later known as the "growth factor." If the weight of the airplane was thoughtlessly increased by one kilogram, we must increase the strength of various parts to support the increased weight, and this would mean additional weight increases which, in the case of a fighter, would also equal about one kilogram. At the very least, then, the first one kilogram increase would result in a two kilogram increase. Because these changes further increased the weight supported by the wing, the wing area must also be larger, which meant another weight increase of several hundred grams. This would reduce performance unless we used a more powerful engine. Even without a new engine, unfavorable conditions would proliferate, one after the other, such as the final weight increase, a drag increase because of the bigger wing, and material and manufacturing problems. Therefore, we had to be most careful to maintain weight control, and I was constantly reminding myself and the other members of the design team of this crucial fact. I was certain this policy must be followed more strictly than ever before. On top of that, some new ideas must materialize.

At the early stage of the Prototype 12 concept, I knew we must explore one step deeper and attempt to shine a ray of light where now there was only darkness. Only by departing from traditional customs and specifications could this be accomplished. I felt at that stage of the project that such a philosophy was essential.

By 1932, a new standard called "Summary of Airplane Planning" had been established which had to be adhered to in airplane design. It contained a rule that called for a safety factor prescribing the strength of structural members. This safety factor was defined as the ratio of an airplane's destructive load to the maximum load it was expected to be subjected to during operations. According to the regulation, this factor must be 1.8 regardless of the type of airplane, the application of the force, or the material characteristics. In other words, the rule required the airplane not to be destroyed by loads less than 1.8 times the maximum load experienced in flight. For fighters, the maximum load had been established as seven times the force of gravity, or 7 Gs. Thus, when the 1.8 factor was applied to this, all airplane parts must be able to withstand a load of 12.6 Gs. Even when the airplane went through a maneuver of 7 Gs, which was the maximum load to which it would be subjected, the strength of all parts must have additional capability equal to about 5.6 Gs.

From my past experience in witnessing structural tests, I knew that different materials fail in different ways. If you push on the ends of a long post or a thin plate, you will notice the piece bends more as you increase the force. At the beginning, when the load is small, the part returns to its normal shape when the load is removed. But if you should further increase the magnitude of the force, the part will break at some critical limit beyond which it cannot carry load. The important thing to notice is that this type of structure will be able to regain its original shape almost up to the point at which it fails.

This means the maximum load which can be carried without causing destruction is close to the destructive load. On the other hand, parts in tension that are made to carry axial tension loads, or short stubby compression members, will be permanently deformed at load levels somewhat lower than their destructive load limits. In such cases, the allowable repetitive maximum force is not anywhere near the destructive force.

These two different destruction mechanisms suggested to me a way of reducing the weight of the Prototype 12. Let us assume we make two different types of parts which will both break under a force of 10 Gs. The long, thin part can carry a load of about 9 Gs, very close to the 10 G limit, while still retaining the capability of recovering its original shape. But, on the contrary, the tension parts or stubby compression parts can carry a load of only about 6 or 7 Gs before permanent damage occurs. This means if we use these two parts in an airplane that will be subjected to a maximum load of 6 or 7 Gs, the long, thin part will have excess strength. "This is it," I realized, "I can lower the safety factor for parts that have such excessive strength." As I considered the facts of the matter, it seemed unreasonable to require a uniform safety factor of 1.8 for slender parts just because 1.8 was required for stubby compression parts or tension parts. The airplane's weight could be reduced if the concept of a uniform safety factor were reevaluated. Since there are many slender parts in an airplane, I concluded that a safety factor of about 1.6 was satisfactory for them. After the war, the safety factor was lowered to 1.5 throughout the world, in effect confirming the correctness of my observation. Unfortunately, at the time we did not have time to challenge or argue with the existing worldwide requirement. For slender parts on the Prototype 12, we initiated a moderate policy of using a safety factor slightly below 1.8, and even though I could not calculate the total airframe weight reduction resulting from this policy, I was confident that a considerable amount of weight would be saved. With this breakthrough, I felt there was hope that the Prototype 12 would meet its goals.

Of course, our efforts to reduce weight were made in all areas. For example, sometimes earlier we had considered designing the wing

When I found that some parts had excessive strength if made according to the existing standard, I carefully reduced their weight by redesigning them to a different standard.

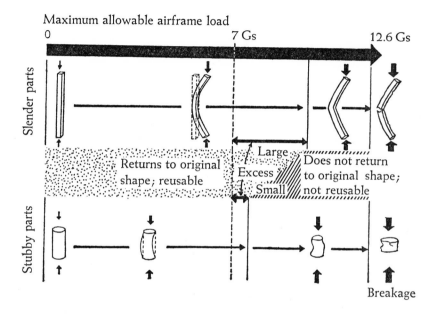

of the Prototype 9 as a single unit from root to tip, instead of inboard and outboard sections. This technique would eliminate the need for heavy attachment fittings on the wings. Although the idea had not been applied to the Prototype 9, we decided to use it for the Prototype 12. Nakajima had already incorporated this technique into its Army Type 97 fighter.

WE NEED LIGHTER MATERIALS

In our weight reduction program for the Prototype 12, the type of material used was a critical consideration. What improvements could be made to increase the strength of existing duralumin? Was there perhaps a lighter, better material we could use? These questions were constantly in my mind. Then, one day, Mr. Kimura, the materials procurement engineer, dropped in to see me. "Mr. Horikoshi," he said, "I have heard that Sumitomo Metals is about to complete the development of a very strong aluminum alloy."[1] According to him, Sumitomo was at the stage of entering experimental production after having developed a higher strength material by slightly changing the composition of an existing duralumin. I was very excited about this information and asked Sumitomo for more details. The Sumitomo man in charge of the project told me about it and invited me to visit the factory. I rushed to Osaka and examined the new material. As I listened to the explanation of the Sumitomo engineers, I knew we could use the new alloy. I also asked them what problems we must watch out for when we used it.

Assuming the material was employed only in the wing spar, I estimated roughly thirty kilograms of weight could be saved. We requested permission to use the new material from Aeronautics Head-

1. Translators' note: This material, referred to as "Super Ultra Duralumin" or sometimes "Extra Super Duralumin" (ESD), was a zinc aluminium alloy equivalent to modern day 7075 material. Its strength properties were significantly higher than those of the normally used copper aluminum alloys, while its unit weight was almost the same. Allied aircraft did not use a similar material until the mid-1940s.

quarters; the Navy was apparently aware of this material and was about to permit its use. Our request was quickly approved.

In addition to the large-scale weight reductions, I did not neglect a single gram even in minor parts. For example, one day a new engineer finished a drawing showing a piece of hardware located in the wing to support the aileron control mechanism. Instead of approving his drawing, I wrote detailed instructions on the outside margin telling him to do it over because I thought we could save 40 percent of the weight by using an aluminum alloy part instead of welded steel. I said 40 percent, but this only amounted to about seventy-five grams, or 1/30,000 of the airplane's final weight. Nevertheless, it was our policy to control anything heavier than 1/100,000 of the airplane's final weight.

The following does not relate to weight, but I recall, one day, a drawing was submitted by a young, inexperienced aide from the structures group. Soon, I discovered that a pulley support for a control cable was directly attached to the fuselage outer skin. It is a basic rule of structural design to attach such members directly to a fuselage frame or else "it's like trying to hang a picture on a curtain." The number of drawings required to manufacture the Prototype 12 airframe was over 3,000. I had to examine and check the entire set of drawings. They were completed in about ten months, and during this time I also had to give detailed instructions and make modifications as required.

A Refined Aerodynamic Design

In parallel with the weight reduction program, we worked in aerodynamic design to improve the stability and control of the airplane and to reduce drag where possible. The airframe was completely refined aerodynamically in order to increase its speed and range as well as improve dogfight performance. First, I made the fuselage somewhat longer than required so as to better withstand the recoil of the 20-mm cannons, thus making the airplane a better gun platform. I used a streamlined canopy to cover the cockpit and provide the pilot with all-around visibility. Next, I had to select the wing airfoil shape, but I had already decided at an early stage of the project to use the Mitsubishi 118. This was our improved version of the airfoil that had been used on the Type 96; it had the best characteristics of any produced by Mitsubishi at that time.

The next issue to be dealt with was the troublesome problem of wing area. It was almost taboo to select a small wing for an airplane such as the Prototype 12 which would be required to carry heavy loads—large quantities of fuel, 20-mm cannons, retractable landing gear, and so forth. In professional language, this would be combining high wing loading with high power loading. Such an airplane would have poor climbing characteristics and would require long airstrips for takeoff and landing. It also would be unable to make swift maneuvers, thus rendering it ineffective in a dogfight. Nor could it take off from a medium-sized aircraft carrier. So, I decided to provide an ample wing area with a wing span of almost twelve meters, the maximum allowable according to both our experience and foreign data. This permitted me to achieve the Navy's requirements with respect to maneuvering, turning radius, landing, and takeoff performance, but it reduced the aircraft's performance with respect to diving, level flight speed, and lateral maneuverability, because of the increased drag and weight of a larger wing. On balance, I decided to proceed with this plan, since turning radius and takeoff performance had a higher priority. In addition, the larger wing area and the lengthened fuselage would provide more stability when the 20-mm cannons were fired. I planned to improve the airplane's speed by reducing drag— that is, cleaning up the airframe aerodynamically rather than depending on a small wing area.

The wing shape was determined only after we had considered the landing gear retraction mechanism, 20-mm cannon installation, fuel tanks, and other installations. After these items had been decided upon, the outside planform shape was left to the designer's taste. For the Type 96 wing I had used a near elliptical rounded shape, but this time I created a more refined appearance by using a straight tapered leading edge and trailing edge while selecting smart-looking parabolas

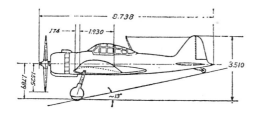

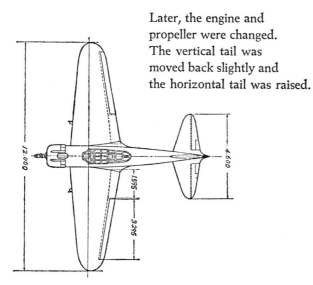

Later, the engine and
propeller were changed.
The vertical tail was
moved back slightly and
the horizontal tail was raised.

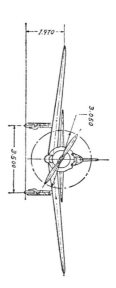

for the wing tips rather than a simple arc. Another item I cannot forget to mention was the wing tip twist. This feature had been used on the Type 96 to improve its fighting performance and I was amazed at its effectiveness. Wing tip twist is provided by twisting the wing so that the angle of attack decreases as you move outboard toward the tip. Since in a tapered wing the stall begins at the tip, it is advantageous to insure that this portion of the wing does not stall first, so that the pilot still has aileron control while at high angles of attack, thus improving dogfight performance. I also used wing tip twist on the Prototype 12 fighter. The amount of twist was so small that it could not be seen simply by looking at the finished wing. After we found it to be effective, we would occasionally say to one another that if Mitsubishi had kept quiet about wing tip twist, no one in the industry would have known the secret of our improved dogfight performance.

I designed the horizontal and vertical tails to satisfy stability and control requirements and was very unhappy with their added weight and drag. But they were there for a purpose and could not be avoided. A large horizontal tail increases longitudinal stability, while a large vertical tail increases lateral stability. An increase in lateral stability should help the pilot when he fires at a target, as would the longer fuselage and larger wing span. Bearing this in mind, we determined the tail area and styled its lines to complement the wing.

Still No Solution to the Problem of Pilot Response

There was still another question that had to be answered while the problems of stability and control were being ironed out. This was how to handle the problem of pilot response—that is, how to regulate the time delay between the pilot's response and the airplane's reaction. The first objective of the pilot, needless to say, is to down the enemy. The airplane must fly precisely as he wishes it to, in order for him to catch the enemy in a crisscross pattern of bullets. As the speed of the airplane increases, if it should resist the pilot's will for even an instant, he could lose his winning chance or even be put at a dis-

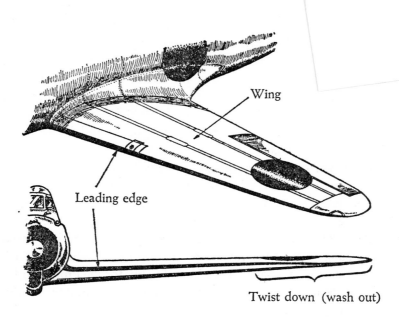

Wing

Leading edge

Twist down (wash out)

Usually, tapered wings stall first at the tip, thereby reducing lateral control. In order to prevent this, a slight downward twist was provided at the tip.

advantage. I had already experienced this problem with the Type 96 fighter; pilots had reported that the Type 96 was faster than any previous fighters by far and was just right at low and medium speeds, but at high speed the elevators were too sensitive and the pilot had to adjust his use of the stick in order to avoid over-controlling. The remedy at the time was to decrease the size of the elevators so as to make them as small as possible without affecting landing performance, which of course occurred at slower speeds. At high speeds, the smaller elevators eliminated the problem for the Type 96 and for airplanes with similar performance.

Later, when I had more time, I conceived a device known as a variable lever ratio unit, which at the pilot's command changed the ratio between the motion of the stick and the elevator's response and displacement. It was effective, but not suitable for fighters. In combat, a fighter pilot's attention was occupied every second, and he could not be changing the lever ratio every time his speed changed. Such a device was not necessary for the Type 96, but for the Prototype 12, I had to come up with a totally new way to decrease elevator sensitivity at high speeds. However, it would take another year for a solution to flash into my mind.

In addition to this, many other new ideas were implemented. For example, in order to increase range, we utilized the existing concept of a detachable auxiliary fuel tank. The tank was designed for low drag and could easily be dropped. It was used during the first leg of a flight and would be dropped prior to the start of a dogfight. This external drop-tank, which had a calculated capacity and streamlined contour, was the first of its kind in the world.[2]

Coming up with these ideas was hard work, but it was also rewarding to see our accomplishments. The design progressed step by step. Our competitor, Nakajima Aircraft, had declined to continue in the competition, while we were deeply involved in our studies. I was fully

2. Translators' note: There were other aircraft, such as the Curtiss Hawk III, that predated the Prototype 12 and also used a drop-tank. Dr. Horikoshi's statement reflects his belief that the integrated configuration of an external fuel tank and the airframe was done for the first time during preliminary design of the Prototype 12.

aware of the problems the Nakajima design staff was facing. Despite our utmost efforts, we were not completely confident we would be able to meet the performance requirements. For the time being, Mitsubishi's Zuisei engine was selected as our power plant, even though its performance had not been perfected. Also, the constant speed propeller was not expected to be perfected, although the manufacturer was desperately attempting to develop the required technology. In short, the engine performance did not live up to our hopes and the constant speed prop was not available! It seemed as though we would not be able to meet *any* performance requirements if we continued in our attempt to bring every performance category to the level of the Navy requirement. To my mind, we were still haunted by the same problems which had caused such difficulty and despair at the early stages of the design. The requirements of extreme maneuverability, speed, and range were simply incompatible, and I desperately needed to know which of these items was more important to the Navy.

DRAWINGS ARE MADE ONE AFTER THE OTHER

The design work of the Prototype 12 progressed through a set sequence of phases despite the problems we faced and changes required. Judging from the condition of the escalating war with China, it was imperative to perfect the new fighter at the earliest possible moment. In the Mitsubishi wind tunnel, tests were completed using the one-eighth scale model which had been manufactured on the basis of the previously completed three-view drawings. The results of the tests were incorporated into the design and were reflected in the production drawings from which the final airplanes would eventually be made. These production drawings went from the design group to the planning and inspection groups. Naturally, there is a sequence in assembling an airplane. The design group releases the drawings according to the assembly sequence and the time interval required to assemble the parts. The planning group first submits a request to the design group specifying the sequence in which the drawings are to be dispatched. Planning also controls the drawings after receiving them, and eventually sends them to each relevant production group. Each production group manufactures the airplane's parts by machining, drilling, pressing, or bending according to the drawings. The parts are then sent to the prototype assembly plant where final assembly takes place.

Aside from this work, those in the inspection group act as judges to make sure the assemblies are carried out according to the drawings received from the design group. It was in the early spring, March 1938, when the drawing of the main wing spar, which was necessary at the beginning stage of construction, was released to the planning group as drawing number 1.

Subsequently, more drawings were made and meetings were frequently held among various people concerning the drawing release schedule. The practical man in charge of the prototype assembly plant was Mr. Naokazu Yui, who had joined Mitsubishi at the same time I did. He would seek whatever leeway he could in the manufacturing schedule, while pressing us for the release of drawings which, as might be expected, tended to be late from time to time. At times, we delivered drawings that had not been completely checked, because the prototype assembly plant wanted a particular drawing before others. Surely, our heads and hands were fully occupied during those busy times.

Maneuverability, Speed, or Range?

While we were busy with the project, time continued to quietly slip by, and suddenly it was April 1938. There had been no time for us to notice the blooming and falling of cherry blossoms. On 13 April, a meeting called "The Council on the Prototype 12 Fighter Plan" was held at Yokosuka Naval Aeronautical Establishment. In the Navy, the Aeronautical Establishment conducted basic inspections and tests of both domestic prototypes and also imported airplanes and their associated armaments. It was customary for the Yokosuka Air Corps to perform operational tests as requested by the Aeronautical Establishment. The combined reports and opinions of these two organizations were used to form an official military appraisal, and a man selected from many top test pilots was appointed to be the chief of flight test for these two groups.

Prior to this meeting, a description of the Prototype 12 fighter plan had been submitted by our company to the Navy, and the first paragraph of our planning policy document had been separately dispatched to the concerned groups by Mr. Hattori. I had personally written the paragraph after considerable deliberation. In it I stated that considering the present level of our aeronautical technology, an effort and way of thinking beyond existing "common sense" were needed to achieve the weight reduction goals and to design a fighter that would fulfill the performance requirements. We also requested that the Navy revise its method of pricing the airplane from one based only on size and weight to one that considered the airplane's usefulness and worthiness.

Pilots were represented at the meeting by Lt. Comdr. Takeo Shibata, a member of the fighter specialist group; Asst. Lt. Kiyoji Sakakibara of the Aeronautical Establishment; fighter commander Lt. Comdr. Minoru Genda; divisional officer Lt. Shigeru Itaya; carrier bomber divisional officer Lt. Masatake Okumiya of the Navy's Yokosuka Air Corps; and others. After explaining the details of the design, I laid down the problems which had been my headache from the beginning. "As you can see, without the constant speed propeller, and without the engine performance improvement, if we try to approach the average values of requested performance, we can't help but lower the speed to about 15 km/hr less than what was requested. And the maneuverability will be less than the Type 96–2 model 1. It is a different story if the engine performance and the reliability of the constant speed propeller can be improved." To this I added, "I would like to hear your opinions on the priorities of importance among the qualities of range, speed, and maneuverability." After listening to my talk, Lieutenant Commander Genda, who was paying very close attention to me, took a big drink of tea and then stood up to give his opinion. In a clear, solid tone of voice he said, "The Type 96 fighter is able to win in the dogfights mainly because of its maneuverability. Of course the requirements must surely be met but if

I have to answer Mr. Horikoshi's question, I think we should put the first priority on maneuverability. I believe we must sacrifice some of the range and speed, if necessary, in order to obtain maneuverability." I took that as an expression of his confidence in my judgment. But there was an opposing opinion as well. Lieutenant Commander Shibata of the Aeronautical Establishment stood up, saying, "Objection!"

Six years earlier, when I went to the Aeronautical Establishment on some other business, Commander Shibata told me he believed a low-wing monoplane was not suited for crisscross dogfights, thus making its use as a fighter doubtful. But three years later, when I met him at the tests of the Type 96, he came up and apologized by saying, "I previously was very impolite simply because of my ignorance; I wish to apologize." He looked resolute but determined—the unique fighter pilot and at the same time a typical sincere soldier.

Now Commander Shibata spoke as follows: "As you can see in the combat reports from the Sino-Japanese War, damage to our bombers by enemy fighters has been greater than expected. We must protect the bombers with long-range fighters; and also, to catch the fleeing enemy, we must fly slightly faster. I think the shortcomings of maneuverability can be compensated for by better control of the airplane—in other words, training. But even a pilot with fighting spirit and excellent skills cannot make his airplane fly faster than its maximum design speed. He will also find it difficult to fly farther than the maximum design range. Therefore, I believe we should emphasize speed and range rather than maneuverability."

Then Commander Genda stood up and hot arguments flared between the two. No one at the meeting could have declared a winner of the arguments, and neither one wanted to compromise. As I listened to them, I thought, "The opinions of these two are both correct in someone's mind; therefore, the dispute will continue forever. To stop such an inconcludable argument, there is nothing to do but to produce a machine that meets all requirements. As for me, I must thoroughly reconsider the weight reduction and aerodynamic requirements that evolved from the previously settled design policy, and I must try to accelerate the development of both the constant speed propeller and improved engine performance." I decided this was the only way out; there would be no other way.

It Is Big but It Looks Good

Soon after the 27 April meeting, the inspection of the full-scale mock-up took place at the prototype assembly plant at Mitsubishi. Starting from this point, our Prototype 12 would undergo many inspections and tests from every angle until its first flight. It would be trained to become a fine young warrior.

The full-scale mock-up, which had been completed for this day, was a model having exactly the shape and size of the finished airplane. It was built off in a corner of the plant prior to the manufacturing of the actual prototype. Wood was mainly used to construct this highly detailed mock-up, and a dummy engine and armament were installed. The object of building the mock-up was to provide a tool with which inspections and instructions for modifications could be made if necessary, so that the user would be satisfied with the final product. Such items as the outside contours, cockpit, engine surroundings, installed equipment, instrument panel, landing gear, control systems (including detailed parts and associated framework), strength and locations of inspection panels, pilot's visibility, and suitability for operation, inspection, and maintenance were considered. On this day, visitors from the Navy were Captain Kira, the chief of the Aeronautical Establishment's flight test division and about ten others, including Lieutenant Itaya of the Yokosuka Air Corps and Lieutenant Commander Shibata. Since the Prototype 12 had caused such heated arguments day after day, the Navy men must have been anxious to see the full-scale mock-up as soon as possible. I was also anxious to hear the pilots' first impressions of the new design.

The pilots went to the prototype assembly plant as soon as they arrived, without spending much time in greetings. As they entered the building everyone said, "It is quite big." In general, fighter pilots worry about the size of their airplane and it is easy to understand why the Prototype 12 appeared to be big, since its span was one meter greater and its fuselage one and one-half meters longer than the Type 96 fighters which the pilots were just getting accustomed to flying. I remembered my correct intuition of six months ago; there had been no other choice but to use the smaller engine. Even with this small engine, the airplane was considerably bigger than the Type 96. But if I had used a bigger power plant, the airplane would have been yet one size bigger than it was now. After walking around the mock-up, the pilots commented, "It is a smart-looking airplane, isn't it?" Contemplating the mock-up, which seemed filled with speed and dynamic sense, I looked at Mr. Hattori and we grinned at each other; we enjoyed hearing the pilots' typically straightforward remarks.

After a brief exterior inspection, Commander Shibata climbed into the cockpit. He examined the location of the stick and various other control levers, instruments, and machine guns for suitability of use by the pilot. Then Lieutenant Itaya took his turn. As they whispered to each other on important points, they listed problems on a blackboard provided for that purpose. The inspection took about two hours, and when it was concluded, there were over one hundred instructions for improvements, including the relocation of some minor parts. One hundred items may seem like a lot, but this was not unusual for a mock-up inspection. Thus, the designer and the pilots who would actually use the aircraft consulted each other from time to time; this was the only way to produce a comfortable, easy to handle airplane. Needless to say, we started to make the suggested changes the same day.

Work on the Prototype Begins

By then, the comfortable, early summer season had passed and it was steaming hot weather in Nagoya. Design work was in full swing; drawing release and the manufacture of parts were coming along well. I can still remember the times I had to wipe my sweaty hands as I checked various drawings. During the lunch hour break, I used to enjoy watching the kayaks and skulls in the ship channel adjacent to The south edge of the plant. Finally, the actual assembly of the Prototype 12 began in the fall when the ocean breeze from Ise Bay began to make things a little more comfortable. Previously, the trial manufacturing had been carried out in a temporary location at the production plant, but for the Prototype 12 the big building across the field from the main building which housed the design room was utilized as the prototype assembly plant. Prior to assembly, frameworks called jigs were securely mounted to the floor, and in them the three major subassemblies—the wing, forward fuselage, and aft fuselage—were assembled. In the case of the wing, three spars which ran the length of the wing would be loaded into the jig, and airfoil-shaped webs, called ribs, were placed perpendicular to the spars and firmly fastened in place so as to form the shape of the wing. It would take several months to complete each subassembly. During that time, the jig must hold everything in its proper location; hence the jigs were made of heavy-gauge steel pipes.

One day, after about one third of the scheduled drawings had been released, I visited the prototype plant and it happened that manufacturing personnel were inspecting the accuracy of the jigs. For checking the straight and horizontal lines, they were using an instrument which looked similar to those used in land surveying. The position of each member was checked and adjusted as deemed necessary. After these paintaking preparations were made, the three main spars were loaded into the jig and the ribs were then installed. When I followed the contour formed by the small ribs spaced about twenty-five centimeters apart, sure enough, there appeared the shape of the wing we had made on the drawings.

Meanwhile, a short distance away, the fuselage jigs were mounted on the floor, the forward and aft sections being built separately. On these jigs were a number of frames which looked like slices of fuselage, neatly arranged in order of size and resembling an ancient animal skeleton. In addition to the manufacturing of this first flying prototype, construction was under way on a test airplane that would be subjected to vibration and strength tests by the Navy. The plant crew was also getting ready to assemble the jigs for a second prototype.

A Disturbance within the Navy

In the prototype plant, the landing gears, which would be retracted after takeoff and stored in the wing, and the hardware to support the 20-mm cannons were being attached to the wing of the number one prototype. The riveting of the wing skins had also begun, starting from the tips and moving inboard. In the factory, the noise of riveting was so loud that we had to shout to carry on conversations. As for the fuselage, which was being assembled separately from the wing, its frames were already in the jigs and longitudinal structural members were awaiting the application of the external skins. Jigs to assemble the ailerons, tails, and flaps were almost complete and were located in a corner of the plant.

I cannot forget the unexpected change in the Navy's plans which could have ended the smoothly operating design and manufacturing process of this project. It amounted to a fundamental objection to the design policy of the Prototype 12, and had originated within the Navy. Several months earlier, the Navy had started to reinvestigate all previous airplane types as well as new types in development. This investigation stemmed from reports of various problems with different airplane types and methods of air combat and attack. The study was based on the expertise and experience of the Japanese military forces during the early stages of the Second Sino-Japanese War. The Yokosuka Air Corps and the Twelfth Air Corps, stationed at the front lines in China, were asked to submit their opinions to the Navy authorities. Some of the suggestions resulting from these opinions were good and appeared feasible, but I particularly noticed the widespread opposition from the frontline military personnel to the concept of the Prototype 12. Since this opinion was voiced by the most powerful corps in the Navy, which had a great deal of influence, it was a shock to me as the chief designer. For example, suggestions such as the following were submitted: "We should manufacture fighters specialized in local air defense. We should concentrate on maneuverability instead of range for fighters based away from the front lines. We need twin-engine fighters for long-range escorts. We should design an airplane equipped with machine guns that fire in all directions for the sole purpose of escorting long-range, land-based bombers."

Among these suggestions, the idea of specialized local defense was correct, but the notion of using both carrier-based fighters and twin-engine fighters would divide the performance we were trying to build into the Prototype 12. As for the concept of long-range escort bombers, it was so ridiculous I thought that whoever suggested it must believe an airplane's speed and maneuverability were about the same as that of a battleship. Other criticisms were also voiced. In the opinion of the Twelfth Air Corps, "20-mm cannons installed in the wing have only disadvantages and no advantages." This opinion made me feel especially uneasy, since I was not experienced in selecting armaments. Besides, if the Navy authorities viewed these various opinions as being important and took any action to alter our plans for the Prototype 12, all of our previous efforts would be in vain and the Japanese Navy would suffer a great loss. My honest feeling was that they could not do that to us now.

In the middle of October, soon after I learned about the mood of the Navy, I went to see Lt. Comdr. Eiichi Iwaya, who was in charge of fighters for the Naval Aeronautical Headquarters in Tokyo. I wanted to exchange opinions with him about the new fighter program which would follow the Prototype 12. When I expressed my views on the suggestions made by the Yokosuka Air Corps and the Twelfth Air Corps, Commander Iwaya was quite agreeable. I felt relieved when he said I could disregard the Twelfth Air Corps' opinion concerning the 20-mm cannons. But he asked me to be fair and make a performance estimate for a carrier-based fighter designed strictly for maneuverability which followed the suggestions of the Twelfth Air Corps. Upon returning to Nagoya, where I was continuing design work, I managed to make a performance estimate as requested by Commander Iwaya.

I left out the 20-mm cannons, reduced the range, decreased the wing span and wing area accordingly, and found weight could be reduced about 15 percent, thus improving maneuverability. This airplane would certainly be accepted at the outset by the majority of the pilots as a successor to the Type 96, but I could not help thinking its life would be short. Also, there was very little margin in the airplane to improve its performance in the future by replacing its engine with a more powerful unit.

On the other hand, the Prototype 12 with its 20-mm cannons, extremely long range, and other high levels of performance could be used for some time to come as a superior fighter, an escort, and an attacker. Meanwhile, we could gain time to develop a more specialized fighter for local combat purposes. I believed this to be a much more realistic way of thinking and, furthermore, I believed more firmly than ever that the only way to win military victories, since we lacked resources and manpower, was to concentrate on developing a small, high-quality military force.

I told myself, "All right, if the Navy wants me to change the plan, I shall spell out, without hesitation, what I truly believe. If they don't accept this, I'll worry about it then." This helped me to settle down. When I talked to Mr. Hattori, who at that time was the head of engineering and also the chief of the first design section, he listened and silently smiled, as if to say, "Don't worry about it." This gave me courage. I did not tell anyone on the design team except Mr. Sone and Mr. Hatakenaka, because I feared a loss of morale would result.

At that time, we were in the midst of stress analysis, drawing preparation, and strength testing of parts. With the preliminary results of wind tunnel testing completed, the unknown elements of the design were eliminated, one by one, and this gave us encouragement. It was similar to what a mountain climber might experience when the mountain top which had originally been covered by clouds when he started his climb breaks into view in the near distance. Accordingly, I gradually began to feel that the objectives we had strove so hard to obtain were now within our grasp.

After that, as might have been expected, the Aeronautics Headquarters did not add any more changes to the Request of Plan. But somehow I felt the enthusiasm in the Navy was cooling off for the Prototype 12 fighter. With the completed product before us, however, the rightness or wrongness of its design concept could actually be proven. Those of us who live in a world of technology should not have to experience joy and sorrow in quick alternation as a result of half-joking criticism or unfounded guesses. I worked with all my might, warning myself not to misjudge what was needed for long-term progress.

Flight Test

THE CONSTRUCTION OF THE PROTOTYPE 12 MAKES STEADY PROGRESS

The New Year's Day holiday of 1939 was the most peaceful period of time I had known in the past six months. In June of 1937 my son was born, but because I had been so busy, I was not able to spend much time with him. Finally, it seemed I would be able to recapture a short period of family life. My son enjoyed it very much when I picked him up and raised him high above my head as we stood on the sunny veranda. During the New Year's holiday of the previous year, my mind had been filled with such questions as, "How am I going to meet the severe requirements for the Prototype 12? Am I really capable of doing it?" These doubts had weighed heavily on my mind like a piece of cold lead. It was quite different now. There were still many problems to solve, but the assembly of two flying models had begun and the structural test airframe was making good progress. I flattered myself to think that I had been able to come this far by self-encouragement and the support of all the members of my team.

When the three days of the holiday had passed, I began to travel again to the familiar Mitsubishi plant in Nagoya. Getting off the gaily decorated streetcar and walking for a few minutes down the gravel road to my office, I visualized the new fighter as a silver-winged bird still sitting on the floor of the factory, unable to fly. I knew I must give this bird its soul as soon as possible.

58

The first job of the new year was to deliver the test airplane to the Naval Aeronautical Establishment where strength and vibration tests would be made. The strength capabilities of the airframe would be determined by test load conditions which simulated many maneuvers, such as tight turns and inverted flight pullouts. The vibration tests were required to gather data such as the airplane's natural frequency, so that the critical flutter speed could be determined and studies could also be made concerning resonance with the engine, propeller, and airframe. These tests were very important and I was anxious to learn the results. In particular, the strength testing was of interest, since it would prove or disprove my theory of the reduced safety factor.

When I dropped in at the prototype plant, the test airframe and the first flying model were all ready to be assembled by joining the subassemblies, such as the wing, fuselage, and tail. Sections of the number two flying model were still in the process of assembly in the jigs. A few days later, first the test airframe and then the number one Prototype 12 subassemblies underwent final assembly. After one and one-half years, the new fighter removed its cloak of secrecy and revealed its fierce elegance. I was not able to witness the final assembly, but later, when I visited the plant, I saw the airplane in its almost finished state. Still unpainted and displaying a few machine and tool marks, the naked airplane appeared to overpower the plant with its shiny metal skin.

The first two prototypes would one day spread their wings in the sky, but for the test airframe, which was dimensionally and structurally identical to them, a less pleasant fate was in store, since it would undergo strength tests to the point of destruction after the vibration tests were finished.

Several days later, after completing most of the remaining work, Mr. Sone and I went to Yokosuka to make arrangements for the delivery of the test airframe to the Aeronautical Establishment. We also wanted to talk about the tests with those from the airplane and science divisions who would be in charge of conducting them. Skipping the usual holiday greetings, these men, whom I already knew, quickly began to ask questions about airframe tests and the status of work on the prototypes. It appeared they had waited a long time for this opportunity.

As I was making final arrangements for the tests, the finishing touches were being put on the number one Prototype 12. When Mr. Sone and I returned to Nagoya, most of the preparations for delivering the test airplane were complete. After a few additional modifications, which resulted from our visit to Yokosuka, the test airframe was disassembled into two sections and loaded on a freight train.

WE PASS THE FIRST TEST

About two weeks later I heard from representatives of the Aeronautical Establishment. They said the results of the vibration test, as well as some other tests, were soon to be released. The next day I visited their offices and met with Mr. Kiyoshi Matsudaira of the airplane division. It was he who had the file of the test results. Mr. Matsudaira, a graduate of the University of Tokyo, was originally a naval engineer. He was younger than I, and later he would be known as the greatest authority on vibration problems not only in the Navy but in all of Japan. A tall man with an aristocratic appearance, Mr. Matsudaira said, "Mr. Horikoshi, the results of the vibration tests look very good," and he proceeded to report the findings in a businesslike way in his usual calm voice. According to his report, after tests were made on the airframe we had supplied as well as on a wing flutter model, he estimated the flutter speed to be much higher than the 900 km/hr calculated by Mitsubishi. This meant the airplane would be less prone to flutter than we had originally believed and should be quite safe. For me, these results were good news and were much better than expected. The strength tests were scheduled to take place after the vibration tests were complete, and it would be a few months until they would be finished.

We were instructed by Mr. Imanaka of the Aeronautical Establishment science division to make a slight change in the tail location for future production aircraft and, as a stopgap measure, to add a small fin on the underside of the aft fuselage on the first two prototypes.

This modification was the result of wind tunnel tests on the spin model performed by the Navy. Needless to say, I was sorry to add such a thing to my refined, smart-looking aircraft, but it could not be helped if it was necessary.

Among the results given to us that day, those that related to flutter remained firmly implanted in my mind. At the time, I was not at all suspicious of the conclusions derived from the tests, but they would lead to a sad experience and a terrible accident later on. But no one was aware of this at the time. Theoretical studies of airplane flutter were not sufficiently advanced for this fighter, since its speed and capabilities were considerably higher than those of previous airplanes. It would take two more years and the precious life of a brave man to unveil the problems hidden in the results of the tests.

FINALLY, THE NUMBER ONE PROTOTYPE 12 IS COMPLETE

The Prototype 12 was rapidly approaching its completion and Mitsubishi announced that the completion inspection would be conducted on 17 March 1939. While we called it a completion inspection, there were still various minor things to be done inside, and there was no accurate estimate of how long these minor adjustments would take. During this period of final work, we selected a date for the overall inspection to be performed. Such a ritual was traditional as a milestone to measure a project's progress, and there would be no other day as dramatic and emotional as the final completion inspection day for the design staff and people working in the prototype shops. As I look back, I am grateful to all who worked so hard as a team to overcome the objections raised by the Navy, while enduring the strain and restlessness caused by the uneasy feelings we experienced.

The finished prototype was painted a dimly-shining ash green except for the engine cowling, which was black. As I looked at my new fighter, there was no doubt it was one size bigger than the Type 96, but it was beautiful with its trim wing arranged in straight lines and the well-balanced position of its tail. The fuselage was streamlined from the cowling to its aftmost point. The only dissatisfaction I felt was with the small fin that had been added to improve the spin recovery characteristics. But, other than that, the image I had had at the early stage of conception had now finally become reality through the medium of thousands of drawings. To witness the two-dimensional drawings turn into a three-dimensional article, which now stood in front of me, caused a deep emotion which the other designers also shared. The fuselage felt hard and cold to my touch. It had not yet been baptised by the airstream or the hot exhaust gases from its engine, but standing on the factory floor it looked as though it wanted to leap into the sky and I could almost hear the roar of its engine.

The completed prototype was subjected to its inspection in the presence of the Navy inspector stationed at Mitsubishi. This included weighing the airplane, determining its center of gravity, verifying its major dimensions, verifying left-right symmetry, determining the range of control surface movement, and verifying the operation of systems such as the power plant.

Among other things, after the prototype was complete, the designer's primary interest would be to see if the weight goals had been met. Of course, the original weight estimate had been refined many times, but the final figure must come from weighing the aircraft. It had been one year since we had submitted our description of "Planning for the Prototype 12," and every member of the design staff had endeavored to reduce the aircraft's weight wherever possible, as could be seen by an inspection of the drawings. It was very difficult to reduce airframe weight, but we tried so hard that instead we reduced our own body weight! I studied every method of weight control one could imagine, from our adventurous technique of reducing the uniform safety factor to using the most modern materials such as the Ultra Duralumin, which in itself became a landmark in Japanese aviation technology. Such long and determined efforts to reduce weight were about to be judged and we would soon see if our original objective had been achieved.

There were scales in the corner of the prototype plant. Two scales were mounted on a pair of rails so they could be freely moved when needed, and they were also capable of measuring the weight of airplanes with different wheel treads. A third scale was designed to be placed under the tail wheel. The weight obtained from the scale readings was used to find the airplane's center of gravity, and when the three values were added together, they gave the weight of the airplane. The Prototype 12 was pushed onto the scales and the tail wheel scale was put in place. Crew members were stationed at each scale station and, momentarily, there was silence. Those who were breathlessly staring at the motion of the scale indicators suddenly began to call out values. I prayed that the numbers I would hear were less than those I had estimated, even if by only one kilogram or even one gram. As a result of adding the recorded values, the weight of the airplane came out to be 1,565.9 kg. I heard a sigh of relief from everyone. According to our year-old estimates it would weigh 1,533.9 kg. But the greater actual weight included a total of 55 kg of excess weight in the Navy-supplied engine, propeller, and landing gear. It was clear there was no excess weight in the airframe, even if we included the weights of some small parts still unmounted, such as support parts for the machine guns. In the long run, this figure showed our efforts were adequately rewarded. When I looked around, I saw three smiling faces looking toward me. They were Messrs. Sone, Hatakenaka, and Tanaka. By their expressions I could tell they were saying to themselves, "We've made it!"

As I look back now, I feel as if we had devoted our daily efforts for many months so as to be able to enjoy that day's short-lived happiness and relief from such a long period of strain. It seemed as though the figures meant nothing to the younger team members, but as soon as we explained the significance of our weight reduction program, they also appeared to be pleased. Later, toward the end of March, at the Kagamigahara hangar just prior to the first flight, the total weight, including every part, fuel, oil, and so forth, turned out to be 1,620 kg, which was 86 kg over the estimate made in our year-old plan description and, as previously mentioned, included 55 kg overweight in the Navy furnished parts. We had exceeded our original projection for airframe weight by only 31 kg. I was completely satisfied.

As a rule in airplane design, performance calculations are always made with a little allowance to account for excess weight. Therefore, if the engine power was according to specification, the birth of an unparalleled fighter was certain. Flight tests would supply the final proof and, as I learned from the inspection reports, such tests were soon to occur.

THE PROTOTYPE IS MOVED TO KAGAMIGAHARA AIRFIELD

About a week after the final inspection, when all necessary work had been finished, the number one Prototype 12 was disassembled into several sections, crated, and removed from the plant at Oye-cho, Minatoku, in the south end of Nagoya city. It was loaded on two ox carts and at a little past 7:00 P.M. on 23 March the caravan set out through Nagoya city into the night. It passed through Komaki and Inuyama, and eventually reached the Mitsubishi hangar at the corner of Kagamigahara airfield, Gifu prefecture, about forty-eight kilometers away. The trip took one full day. I was surprised at the primitive, time-consuming method used to transport an airplane capable of flying several hundred kilometers per hour. The caravan's speed was less than three kilometers per hour. But this procedure was simply the result of the Japanese policy of circumstantial adaptability which had been instituted in the Taisho period to help carry forward the modernization of Japan.[1]

Soon after I joined the aircraft plant of Mitsubishi, I was sent abroad to study the European and American aircraft technologies, and I noticed that every aircraft plant I visited was located next to an airfield. But in those days in Japan only two companies were located near an airfield, Tachikawa Aircraft and the Ohta manufacturing plant of the Nakajima Aircraft Company. The Gifu plant of Kawasaki joined this select group during the Prototype 9 competition. The reason for this inconvenient arrangement was the small proportion of flat land relative to the entire land area of Japan. Most of the flat land available was well cultivated and used as farmland. Undeveloped fields in northern Honshu and Hokkaido were geographically un-

1. The Taisho period was from 1912 to 1925.

desirable as locations for plants of rapidly-advancing technological industries. In general, therefore, most manufacturing plants and airfields were located separately. There also was a logical reason for using an ox cart to transport the airplane, namely, very poor roads. In those days, there were no paved roads leading to the airfields, which were located between Inuyama and Gifu city; most were gravel paths full of dips and turns. What would have happened to an airplane if a truck or a horse carriage were used on such a road? Any light fuselage, made of light metal or wood, most likely would have suffered damage as it rattled around. That was why an ox cart, with its smooth riding characteristics and tight turning radius, was selected. For those times, prior to the Pacific war, it was more than adequate, since we were producing only a few airplanes a day.

The new fighter arrived at the Kagamigahara hangar and went through its last minute preflight inspections, which included trial engine runs, tests of moving parts, minor repairs, maintenance, and measures of weight and center of gravity. The man in charge of the last minute preparations was Mr. Kumataro Takenaka, who also had been responsible for the general arrangements during the manufacture of the prototype. Mr. Takenaka frequently telephoned me at Nagoya to bring me up to date on the airplane's status. On the basis of these calls, specialist technicians could be dispatched along with materials and parts as required. Also, design engineers Mr. Kato (landing gear system) and Mr. Tanaka (power plant) could be rushed to Kagamigahara following the dispatch of parts and technicians. Mitsubishi Engine Manufacturing Plant sent Mr. Izumi as a reinforcement. As the work progressed, 1 April was selected for the maiden flight. This decision was immediately reported to the main office of Mitsubishi and from there to the Naval Aeronautics Headquarters and, eventually, to the Aeronautical Establishment. I could visualize members of all those organizations, who had witnessed many tests, saying, "Finally, it is going to fly." We had been informed late in March that the structural tests showed the airframe could slightly exceed its required loads even with the reduced safety factor. I had followed these tests closely and was relieved to hear the Navy had no objections to the forthcoming flight tests.

At Kagamigahara, Mr. Takenaka performed trial engine runs, and the favorable results meant that the scheduled maiden flight of 1 April was a certainty. As soon as I heard this, I consulted with Mr. Asada, chief of the flight test section, and made an in-house test schedule. It would start with ground operation tests, then takeoff and landings; next special flights would be made, including dives; and finally the external fuel tank would be dropped. The test plan would fill a large notebook and contained seventeen items in all, consisting of fifty or sixty details.

Each item tested specific characteristics and abilities of the airplane. I could not neglect any one of them and prayed all items would score well. In the afternoon of 31 March, Mr. Asada and I left Nagoya together, taking a train of the Tokaido line from Nagoya to Gifu. The weather was our biggest concern. Just before leaving, I checked with the weather bureau and learned that it would be an unquestionably fine day with no wind. That night, we stayed at a small inn in Gifu city. Although it was the end of March, a foot-warmer was in the bed. The air was cold. Mr. Asada and I talked to each other and tried to convince ourselves that the cold night air was surely the sign of fair weather the following day. Sure enough, the sky I gazed into that evening, while standing in the garden of the inn, was filled with stars.

At Last, It Is in the Air!

Daylight brought 1 April, the first day of flight test. As forecast by the weather bureau, there was not a speck of cloud in the sky; it was an exceptionally fine day. When I arrived at Kagamigahara, I went to the hangar and saw the number one Prototype 12 for the first time in about ten days. At this airfield, there was an Army building located between the fields of the Army's First and Second Air Corps. This day, as usual, the Army was conducting flight training programs and was busily using the fields. Our flight test, which would use the fields extensively, must wait until the training was over for the day. Army planes finished their training at 4:00 P.M.

The wind was reported from the west at three meters per second. The sun was in the west approaching the horizon and the weather was still beautiful; there was no sign of any clouds. The white streamer, with its three bright red rings, was flying to the east, showing the wind's direction. The crew rushed into the hangar and rolled out the airplane. For a moment, it sparkled in the spring afternoon sun as it was rolled onto the grass, and chocks were put under the wheels. It faced the west. Crew members stood by their posts and others, like myself, stood some distance from the airplane.

Those present included Navy flight inspector Lieutenant Commander Nishizawa, flight test chief Mr. Asada, designers Mr. Kato and myself, hangar chief Mr. Imai, Mr. Izumi, and others, for a total of about fifteen or sixteen people. I wanted to bring all the members of the design team so they could enjoy the satisfaction of their accomplishments, but their busy schedules would not accommodate this. However, I did make arrangements for each member to be present at the testing of his particular component during the forthcoming days and weeks of flight tests. The test pilots who were scheduled to fly this airplane into the sky for the first time were the veteran pilot Mr. Katsuzo Shima and another rising pilot, Mr. Harumi Aratani. Mr. Shima was an ex-Navy petty officer, third class, and after his discharge he had joined the Naval Aeronautical Establishment and had tested many fighters, including single-engine and twin-engine attack machines as well as other types. He was known for his violent temper, his ability to precisely control an airplane, and his outstanding skill as an all-around pilot. Mr. Aratani, on the other hand, had a different background. He received his flight training in the Navy after graduating from Tokyo Engineering University as an electrical engineer. Being the older and more skillful of the two, Mr. Shima was chosen to be the lead pilot for the first and subsequent tests.

Mr. Takenaka started the engine, and after a careful inspection was made, Mr. Shima, dressed in his flight suit and wearing a parachute, walked up to the airplane. On his right thigh was strapped a pilot's clipboard so he could record test results during flight. The white paper on the board gave the scene the atmosphere of a real test flight. Mr. Shima pulled himself into the cockpit after mounting the small steps on the fuselage. Settling into his seat, he carefully tried out the engine and instruments and studied the movements of the rudders, elevators, and flaps by operating their respective cockpit controls. Soon afterward he glanced at us, slightly raised his left hand, and waved; this was the sign he was ready. The ground crew quickly pulled the chocks and the airplane suddenly began to move across the grass. The wheels bobbed up and down as the landing gear absorbed the roughness of the ground. With its tail gear on the ground and the nose pointing slightly up, the airplane rolled away. As its speed increased, it rolled in a straight line and then turned to the right and next to the left. Occasionally, the brakes were applied and it came to a halt. It ran all over the big airfield in this manner, and soon the ground tests were completed.

The wheel brakes of an airplane are different from those of an automobile, since they can be operated, both left and right, independently of each other. Because there is no steering wheel to change the direction of an airplane on the ground, to steer one must operate the brakes as well as the rudder. If the brakes malfunction, not only is stopping the airplane difficult but ground directional control is hampered.

Mr. Shima returned to the starting point and opened the canopy with the engine still running; in his loud voice he complained about the poor action of the brakes. The crew immediately adjusted them. After completing the ground run for a second time, Mr. Shima reported he was ready for the jump flight. A jump flight involves flying at an altitude of only several meters by speeding up the takeoff roll and landing almost instantly. At 5:30 P.M., with the evening dusk hanging over us, the aircraft started to roll from the east corner of the airfield. The engine sounded determined and was several levels louder than we had heard it before. People turned their eyes toward the Prototype 12 as it dashed directly to the west while trailing a light dust cloud. I was breathlessly watching for the first moment when this airplane, which was born to be in the sky, came into its element.

Its speed increased until it traveled about one quarter of the field's length and, with an even louder roar, it rose gently into the sky, maintaining an altitude of about ten meters as it flashed by in front of us in the twinkling of an eye. After flying about 500 meters, it touched down safely. As the engine noise ceased, in the quiet of dusk I saw the airplane oscillating wildly on the ground, owing to its landing reaction. It turned around at the west end of the field and returned to the starting place with a roar. Mr. Shima effortlessly opened the canopy, lightly stepped onto the wing, and jumped to the ground. As usual, he received everyone's attention and looked a bit shy, which was unlike his daring personality. We all gathered around him. "The effectiveness of all three control surfaces and the balance in all three directions is satisfactory, but the effectiveness of the brakes is unsatisfactory," he reported almost breathlessly. The three control surfaces referred to were the elevators on the horizontal tail, the rudder on the vertical tail, and the ailerons on each side of the main wing. If the stick in the cockpit is pulled backward, the plane raises its nose by raising the elevators, and if it is pushed forward, the plane lowers its nose by lowering the elevators. Moving the stick to the left or right causes the plane to bank to the left or right by the movement of the ailerons. Pushing the floor pedals causes the rudder to deflect in the respective direction, thereby turning the airplane's nose in that direction. With this one flight, the jump flight was completed. Immediately thereafter, it was decided that stability and control tests could be started concurrently with familiarization flights. We repeated an inspection of all parts and made modifications where necessary.

It Is Beautiful

Six low-speed familiarization flights with the gear extended were made by each of the pilots, Mr. Shima and Mr. Aratani, by 12 April. From these tests, the pilots were able to make two important observations: "The control surfaces feel like the Type 96. There was considerable vibration during climb, level flight, and gliding with the engine shut down." The resemblance to the Type 96 was satisfactory, given that the Type 96 had the pilots' highest rating. But at this time I could not yet determine the reason for the vibration unless the Prototype 12, which was designed to fly with its landing gear retracted, was experiencing disturbance with the gear down and the disturbed flow was striking the tail, thus causing the problem. The question was, would the vibration be reduced if the gear was retracted? But this was put aside until the gear-down tests were finished. On 14 April, for the first time, we retracted the gear and started special flight tests such as sharp turns and loops at increased speeds. Up to this time, the number one Prototype 12 had been tested so as to determine its basic characteristics, but from this time on, it would be examined for its qualifications as a fighter.

Mr. Shima climbed into the cockpit and, with a roar, the airplane left the ground. As soon as it took off, the two wheels were folded into the wing just as a crab might hold his prey under his arms. "This clearly makes it a different fighter. Surely this is the picture of a new fighter," I thought.

The elimination of the landing gear changed the Prototype 12's profile to one perfectly suited to the blue sky. The airplane did not look as if it had been rolling over the ground only a few minutes earlier. It repeated climbs and dives at about 2,000 to 3,000 meters altitude and also performed loops and tight turns several times. Each time it went through a maneuver, a high pitched noise sounded throughout the sky and vibrated the spring air, which was sweet with the fragrance of flowers. I was looking into the sky, forgetting my stiff neck, as I joyously felt the vibration of the air all over my body. The airplane was flying delightfully, wildly and daringly, like a young bird which had finally found its freedom. The trim wing cut sharply through the air and reflected the sunlight every time it turned over. I was almost screaming, "It's beautiful," forgetting for a moment, I was the designer.

THE ELUSIVE VIBRATION

Comparing this day's tests with previous flight tests, two problems became obvious. First, the vibrations did not decrease with the gear retracted. Second, the effectiveness of the elevators as well as the force required to move them at low speed was similar to the Type 96, but at increased speeds the elevators were *too* effective even with only a small stick input. For the first problem, vibration, the source might be in the engine and propeller system, but it was not in the airstream, since retracting the gear did not solve the problem. I thought we must pay more attention to this point in the next series of flight tests. During the flights on the next day, 15 April, a few facts relating to vibration came to light. It was found that there were two peaks of vibration level as the engine speed changed and both appeared to be independent of the airplane's forward speed. From this, we deduced that the vibration of the propeller, engine, or both could be in resonance with the natural frequency of the airframe. For example, if you strike a wine glass, it makes a sound because the glass vibrates at a fixed frequency. In this manner, everything has a characteristic vibration at a particular frequency or multiple thereof which is called the object's natural frequency. Therefore, if the engine's frequency and the airframe's frequency were the same, the engine vibration would be transferred to the airframe, causing the airframe to vibrate more than usual. This phenomenon is called resonance. Further, since every object can have more than one natural frequency, because of the multiples which can exist, it would be possible to have coupling at more than one frequency. The solution, we believed, was to modify or change the frequency of the engine propeller system; the quickest way was to substitute a three-bladed propeller for the present two-bladed version.

On 17 and 18 April we switched propellers and made another flight. The results proved our reasoning was correct. According to the pilot's reports, the vibration was reduced to about one-half of its previous level and the airplane with the three-bladed propeller performed satisfactorily. Having discovered the cause of the airframe vibration, we now had to decide whether to use the three-bladed propeller permanently, or continue with the two-bladed unit while seeking other methods to eliminate the vibration. It was at this point that we decided to invite the Aeronautical Establishment's Mr. Matsudaira, an authority on vibration problems, to assist us. After much investigation we learned that softer engine-support rubber dampers would significantly reduce vibration. Additionally, we decided to try a fixed pitch two-bladed propeller, which was different from the constant speed two-bladed unit. The fixed pitch propeller lowered vibration to acceptable levels for most practical purposes, but we rejected this as a permanent arrangement, favoring instead the use of the two-bladed constant speed unit. At the time, we would not give up this idea. But to achieve it we first had to solve the problem of modifying the engine support system.

The problem of elevator response had been deeply rooted in my mind, even as I was involved in the vibration investigation. Results of flight tests conducted on 17 and 18 April decisively indicated that as speed increased, the elevators became much too sensitive and the airplane responded to even the smallest movement of the stick. This phenomenon of excessive elevator responsiveness was a familiar one and was expected to appear as speed ranges increased, but designers and pilots throughout the world simply did not recognize it as a problem. I wanted to be the first to show it could be overcome, and attacked the problem head on. Recalling our experience with the Type 96, I was determined to find a workable solution. On 25 April, less than a month after our first test flight, we began the performance, stability, and control tests on the fully loaded airplane, weighing 2,331 kg. This included the weight of all regular equipment and the three-bladed constant speed propeller. The results of these tests showed the maximum speed to be greater than 490 km/hr, which was a little higher than our estimated value of 480 km/hr. It was later learned that when the airspeed corrections were made, another 18 km/hr would be added, making it possible to virtually equal the 500 km/hr called for in the seemingly impossible planning request.

I Am Challenged to Achieve a Control Response That Matches Human Reactions

By this time, I regarded the first stage of the company's flight test program to be complete. On 1 May, I visited the Navy Aeronautics

Headquarters and the Naval Aeronautical Establishment in Tokyo and Yokosuka to report on our flight test results and discuss future programs using the number one Prototype 12.

At the Naval Aeronautical Establishment, unexpected answers were waiting for me. Normally, as in the case of the Type 96 program, when the company flight tests were largely completed, additional testing would be performed by the government. But this time, after I made my report, the Navy stated it wished to receive the prototype only when we considered it to be ready, since there were still some problems with the airplane and Mitsubishi seemed to be able to find the solutions quickly. When I heard this I thought, "They know what they are doing all right," because some of the alternatives I was considering were unconventional. The Navy officers must have concluded it was quicker for the company to finish the project than to attempt to do it themselves. Also, they must have appreciated the skills and abilities of the Mitsubishi pilots. In spite of this, it was unprecedented to allow the company to finish the stability and control tests, and I was more determined than ever to solve the problem of control response. Also, on this day, the Navy Aeronautics Headquarters gave us permission to install the Nakajima Sakae Type 12 engine in the number three flight test aircraft and it was designated as the A6M2. The letter "A" stood for a carrier-based fighter, the numeral "6" indicated that this was the Navy's sixth carrier-based fighter, while "M" meant Mitsubishi. The numeral "2" indicated this was the second version of Mitsubishi's Prototype 12 fighter. The first two models with the Mitsubishi Zuisei engine were known as A6M1.

Following these meetings with the Navy, I sat down and organized the remaining problems to be solved. First of all, the biggest issue was to improve the elevator control system so that at high or low speed the elevators would be neither too responsive nor too unresponsive. Other than that, there were about five unsolved problems, including a method to control vibration from the two-bladed constant speed propeller; the effectiveness of ailerons at low and high speeds; and, as always, additional weight reduction of the aircraft. But the most important and most time-consuming problem was that of elevator response. Because the fighter's performance during air battles was strongly affected by elevator response, we were obliged to undertake the full course of design modeling and tests. We would have to discover a new solution, design new parts, test them, build a prototype installation, install it on the airplane, and then actually prove it in flight. The problem had attracted my attention during the design stage about one year earlier, and had stayed with me since the beginning of flight tests in April.

The rate of stick motion and the elevator control of previous airplanes was constant at both high and low speeds. The stick and elevator were connected by metal tubes, levers, and cables, and as the stick moved, the elevator moved accordingly. In those days, all parts in the control system were designed to be very stiff; in other words, even if the airload on the elevator changed because of a change in speed, it was considered very poor for elevator motion to change for a given stick motion. Therefore, elevators that could demonstrate suitable effectiveness at low speeds would become excessively responsive at high speeds, and would rapidly change the airplane's attitude. Even at the same elevator angle, the load on the elevator was greater at a higher speed and the airplane's response more violent. If the elevators were designed so as to have a comfortable response at high speeds, they were usually ineffective at lower speeds. The reason this was not yet a major issue was simply that previously designed airplanes did not have a speed range as great as that of the Prototype 12, and skillful pilots could compensate for the control system defect.

Two factors contributed to our awareness of the problem of control response. First, as previously mentioned, the Prototype 12 had a greater speed range than previous models; and, second, our chief test pilot, Mr. Shima, decided to exert his full efforts to improving the aircraft's control mechanism. Not satisfied only to fly the airplane, he also wished to become involved in the solution of development problems. When I began my analysis, it soon became obvious that for a given amount of stick motion the elevators should move only a little at high speed but much more at low speed. They should also move a corresponding distance at speeds between maximum and minimum. My idea for achieving such a desirable solution was to transform the aircraft's speed into elevator load and use this load to change the stick elevator ratio from high to low speed. But I could not find a simple, reliable method to do this at that late stage of the design, and my thinking process came to a halt.

I Have an Unexpected Idea

One day, and I cannot remember exactly when it occurred, an idea flashed into my mind. Could I utilize the elasticity of the control system? The elasticity of a system is the characteristic that causes contraction or expansion according to the magnitude of the applied force. An elastic object will return to its original length or shape when the force is released. This idea came to me suddenly, but perhaps it had been there for a long time. If I made the control system easy to deflect—in other words, if I decreased its rigidity—as the airplane speed increased, airloads would increase on the elevator, and forces in the control system would also increase, causing increased deflections either by bending, expansion, or contraction. Less than normal elevator motion for a given motion of the stick would occur, and as the speed decreased, the reverse would be true. This chain of thought passed through my mind in a moment. However, if such a method were to be used, since the control system would be somewhat elastic, an obvious question was, would there be a delay in control surface system response? Luckily, I did not have to worry about that, because the deflection of metals or solid material would be transmitted from one place to the other very rapidly. "Splendid," I cried to myself, but I could not be sure until flight tests were performed; it just seemed too simple. When I explained the idea to Messrs. Hattori, Sone, and others, momentarily they murmured their doubts. But, it did not take them long to understand the idea and unanimously they exclaimed, "This is interesting, let's try it."

As previously stated, elasticity in the control system was tradi- tionally considered to be undesirable and the standard specification called for a rigid system. In other words, it was standard procedure not to allow any signficant deflection to occur in the control system, although even the number one Prototype 12 did not entirely meet this requirement. Further reduction of control system elasticity would mean that I would have to ignore this standard requirement. I investigated possible detrimental factors which might arise because of a reduction in stiffness of the system. For instance, if I moved the stick fore and aft rapidly, would this excite the airplane and induce a pitching motion which would not be damped? Also, I wondered if the elevators would fail to respond effectively to a small motion of the stick. But these matters could easily be investigated during flight tests. Another question was, would flutter be a problem? I did not think it would, since other studies showed the airplane to be flutter-free.

It was after the Type 96 went into operation that a regulation defining the minimum requirements for control system stiffness became effective. I never heard why this regulation was instituted, but it was true that many fabric-covered aircraft had ineffective elevators. Despite the fact that there was no solid foundation to support the control system, the inability to obtain the required elevator deflections must have been blamed on the springiness of the control system itself. Presumably, the regulation defining stiffness must have been established as the symptomatic treatment for this problem; I could not think of any other reason for it.[2] "Well, it shouldn't be a problem if I ignore this rule for the Prototype 12," I said to myself as I made up my mind. The method to carry out the plan was quite simple. In order to obtain the required stiffness—in other words, to reduce the springiness of the system so as to meet the regulation—some parts had been designed far stronger than necessary; it should be possible to increase the system's springiness by reducing the stiffness of these parts without endangering their strength and fatigue characteristics. If this was not sufficient, I could add springs.

I immediately performed calculations on cables having excess strength relative to the loads they must bear, and finally decided to

2. Translators' note: As speeds increased, dynamic considerations became more important in control system design.

use cable diameters of 3.5 mm and 3.0 mm for the original 4 mm, and tubes of 32 mm in place of the original 50 mm. I was convinced that the smaller cables would sufficiently reduce stiffness while retaining adequate strength and durability. This technique would later be described as the "Improvement of Control Response by the Method of Reduced Stiffness."[3]

Toward the end of May, I submitted progress reports to the Navy on all company flight tests, including the first flight. I particularly emphasized that the success of the Prototype 12 was mainly the result of our weight reduction program. I also clearly stated in writing for the first time the problem of excessive elevator response and explained the solution we had devised, which would reduce control sensitivity at high speeds while allowing adequate low speed control. I pointed out that the size of the horizontal tail could no longer provide a solution to this problem. "It is not merely a question of excessive sensitivity and/or heavy elevators but should be considered a new problem, that is, matching the human sense of motion and the airplane's control response throughout the airplane's speed range. We are considering, as a solution to this problem, adjusting the size of the tail and decreasing control system stiffness considerably below the regulation's lower limit."

LANDMARK PROGRESS IN CONTROL RESPONSE

The new, redesigned parts were ready in early June and were delivered to Kagamigahara airfield. The director of the Navy's Aeronautical Establishment, Vice Adm. Koichi Hanajima, came to Kagamigahara on 5 June to observe flight tests, and on this day, for the first

3. Translators' note: A description of the reduced stiffness control system is contained in Report No. 396, Institute of Space and Aeronautical Science, University of Tokyo, March 1965, entitled "A Research on the Improvement of Piloted Airplanes," by Jiro Horikoshi. Much of the original wind tunnel data is also presented. The NACA Memorandum Report "Preliminary Measurements of Flying Qualities of the Japanese Mitsubishi OO Pursuit Airplane," 5 May 1943, by W. H. Phillips also notes the control system flexibility.

The increased speed of the airplane caused the control surfaces to be oversensitive at high speeds. On the Prototype 12, this problem was solved by using a reduced stiffness control system in which the control cables and support system flexed slightly.

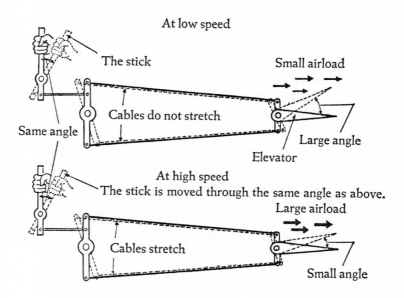

At low speed

The stick

Small airload

Cables do not stretch

Same angle

Large angle

Elevator

At high speed

The stick is moved through the same angle as above.

Large airload

Cables stretch

Small angle

time, we tested the new control system. Mr. Shima and Mr. Aratani were scheduled to fly that day; both of these fine pilots were somewhat nervous during the early stages of the control stiffness program, even though I had already studied the modifications from many points of view and did not believe there would be a really big change in control response. However, the pilots probably thought they were going to test something flimsy. On that day, I had other pressing business and so I sent a young engineer from my staff, Mr. Tojo, to observe the tests at Kagamigahara. I understand that Mr. Shima, as soon as he saw Mr. Tojo, shouted, "What! What happened to Mr. Horikoshi? Get Mr. Horikoshi!" Mr. Shima must have felt it was inexcusable for the chief designer to be absent from the first test of this weird new apparatus. Since Mr. Tojo was put in a difficult position, he phoned me. I could only laugh. Of course I trusted Mr. Tojo completely; that was why I had sent him to Kagamigahara instead of going myself. But it was the outspoken Mr. Shima talking, and I knew that once he started something, he would not withdraw. So, with a smile on my face, I finished the urgent assignment and then hurried off to Kagamigahara airfield.

Sure enough, the tests showed excellent results. As was expected, the amount of stick motion was greatly increased during vertical turns and loops at high speeds. The pilots noted that because of this, the elevator response was softened and flight characteristics were greatly improved. It was also reported that no matter how rapidly the pilot moved the stick, the airplane's oscillations quickly subsided. Hearing these results was a third moment of joy for me; the first occurred on that day in March when the weight measurements were made, and the second on the day in April when the control characteristics were tested. Because Mr. Shima was not the kind of person to be scrupulous about trifles, he candidly approved the success of the new method. Later, when I talked to him about the incident of demanding my presence at the test, he only laughed aloud. How I admired the spirit and boldness of this veteran test pilot!

The results of the reduced stiffness test soon reached the flight test division of the Naval Aeronautical Establishment, and on 12 and 13 June Lieutenant Commander Nakano and Lieutenant Maki from the flight test division were at Kagamigahara for the purpose of making test flights. We had grounded the airplane the day before so that we could give it a thorough inspection. But, unfortunately, on 12 June the airplane was unflyable because of its engine. A spare engine was installed, but it was not in good enough shape to operate satisfactorily. Nor was the airplane ready to fly the next day. The Navy crew complained, but waited two days, spending their time playing bridge or helping to inspect and adjust the engine. In the end, they gave up on the test flight and left. As the manufacturer's representative, I was very embarrassed.

It was typical, in the prewar piston engine days, to waste more than half of the time allocated for flight testing because of engine failures and other difficulties common with prewar engines. This was why some would say that the flight test of the production airplane was, in general, the test of its engine. Engine-related problems continued, but on 6 July the same representatives of the Navy came back and conducted their first official test flights. Taking advantage of this opportunity, we made further reductions in control system stiffness. After flight tests were performed by the four pilots—Mr. Shima, Lieutenant Maki, Lieutenant Commander Nakano, and Mr. Aratani— they all said in one voice, "The elevator response is now satisfactory. There is nothing wrong with this control under any conditions." This solved the biggest problem of our flight testing. I was satisfied that we had been able to match the airplane's control response to the human pilot's sense of motion by making adjustments based on the reports and opinions of our superb pilots. There would be a time in the future when pilots in other countries would desire the same control characteristics; perhaps they would be surprised to know that our pilots and engineers had thought about this problem and solved it prior to the outbreak of the Pacific war. That night, staying in a small inn at Gifu, I could not sleep.

The next day, I asked Commander Nakano and Lieutenant Maki to investigate the vibration of the two-bladed constant speed propeller, which had been a problem since April. As a result of their investigation, I gave up the idea of using a two-bladed propeller and used one of three blades instead.

THE NUMBER ONE PROTOTYPE LEAVES KAGAMIGAHARA

In July, forty-seven flights had been completed, including official flight tests. This large number was partly due to the fact that we were able to keep the engine in good operating condition most of the time; as a result, most of the problems we encountered had been solved. At the conclusion of the second official flight test on 23 and 24 August, the Navy believed that the stability and control characteristics, which had been measured during company flight tests as requested, were almost satisfactory. Problems and failures occurring in the airframe, engine, or other components were nearly all discovered and fixed. Then the Navy issued a statement saying that the airplane would be accepted as soon as the final cleanup, repair, disassembly, and inspections were done. On 13 September the confirmation flight, which was the last flight made at Kagamigahara, was completed. The Navy also announced that the control response characteristics were satisfactory. In comparison to the Type 96, the controls felt light at landing, and they were even more effective than required. One pilot offered his opinion that the airplane's acceleration was too great during dives, and there still remained problems concerning weight and the effectiveness of the ailerons. The fast acceleration in a dive could be advantageous when fighting against a high speed airplane, but I remembered the Navy's opinion that a tight turning radius in a vertical plane was still more important in those days.

In considering the foregoing, it should be clear what a refined control system our military pilots wanted, especially in regard to elevator power and response, which made up the primary control of a three-axis system. We had seriously considered these requests during early design stages, and as a result the control system of the Prototype 12 was efficient at all speeds, with one unit of control stick input resulting in one unit of airplane motion. The pilot no longer had to make continuous fine adjustments according to his speed. As a result, the pilot training period was shortened, and a uniquely refined set of control characteristics was now at the pilot's disposal for use in air battles. This was the successful result of a human engineering approach.

About this time, I gave a lecture at the Naval Aeronautical Establishment on the subject of airplane response, and proposed to the authorities that the regulation governing elasticity of control systems be removed. Although my proposal was not accepted, I discovered after the war that this regulation had been dropped in the United States. This, to my mind, fully vindicated my idea.

About two years earlier, we had first received the Navy's official request for planning, and since the first flight on 1 April 1939, the next four and one-half months had been spent in flight tests. During these months, we had completed 119 flights, totaling 43 hours and 26 minutes of flight time, and 215 separate testing operations on the ground, which totaled 70 hours and 49 minutes. Included in these figures are the tests made to reduce control stiffness. I must say the entire program went quite smoothly. Not only was the problem of control stiffness solved, but the tail size, shape, and control surfaces and systems would not be changed again until the last days of the war. We were able to respond one hundred percent to the Navy's request that the company finish up the stability and control tests. Also, the strength tests, which were conducted concurrently with flight testing, were satisfactorily completed. Among the light structural members having a lowered factor of safety, a few failed slightly below their required strength values. We had expected this and we did not have to impose any flight limitation because they all had factors of safety over 1.6. But we made some minor modifications in order to reach a nominal value of 1.8 for the airplane. This method of selectively increasing strength allowed us to control the weight closely, since there would be no unnecessary structure and some parts would have a safety factor below 1.8 while others would be at or slightly below 1.8.

Thus, on 14 September, the day after the acceptance flight, the first Prototype 12, built by Mitsubishi and piloted that day by Lieutenant Maki, took off at 9:06 A.M. from Kagamigahara airfield, which was still wet with the morning dew. The pilot circled once over the field and flew off to the east; as if saying goodbye, the airplane's wings glittered in the morning sun. As I stood and watched until it disappeared, I could not hold back my emotion. There were tears in the eyes of the design engineers present as well as in those of Mr. Takena-ka and the rest of the maintenance crew who had been involved in the last minute inspections. Young crew members stood by with tears running down their oil-stained faces.

The First
Victim

The First Accident

In the spring of 1940, while Prototype 12s were taking off from Kagamigahara airfield, Japan was becoming deeply involved in the Second Sino-Japanese War, which had started three years earlier in mainland China. Although victorious reports about the Type 96 fighters had been made public until early 1938, now they were no longer heard. The reason for this was that the Chinese air force had withdrawn beyond the range of Type 96 fighters. This often caused serious problems for our unescorted ground troops, and sometimes Chinese planes bombed the front lines. Meanwhile, the news of the Prototype 12's excellent performance reached the frontline troops, and their voices became louder and louder, urging that the new airplane be permitted to join them as quickly as possible. As a result, the Naval Aeronautics Headquarters made arrangements to send the new fighter to the front by the end of April 1940.

Although we were happy to hear this news, having gone through all the ordeals of the trials and flight tests, we still were not completely satisfied with the airplane. The Prototype 12 had not finished all of its operational tests and had begun to show several areas where modifications and additional testing would be required before it was ready to go into action.

About that time, the Navy announced its plans for the Prototype 14 fighter. It was to be a land-based machine whose mission was to attack; later it would become the Raiden interceptor. In the spring of 1940, its design hung heavy on my mind. However, as the outstanding results of the Prototype 12 testing became widely known, I remembered the opposition and uneasiness that had existed within the Navy just one and a half years earlier, and also how happy we had eventually made the Naval Aeronautical Establishment with the Type 96 during its flight testing when it proved to be much better than they had expected. Perhaps, I conjectured, there might be another interesting episode like the one in which the chief naval inspector teased the Naval Aeronautical Establishment while we were working on the Type 96.

The Prototype 12's performance was subject to some criticism. There were those who said that agility was more important than range for a carrier-based fighter and, temporarily, this comment caused the aircraft to be unpopular. To me, this was somewhat funny, in an ironic sense, because extra long range was the feature for which the frontline troops were calling. Honestly, I should not call it funny, since serious problems can result when soldiers in the field change their mind like this.

On 11 March, when I was busily involved with both the Prototype 12 and 14, about 3:00 in the afternoon as I was working away, a young member of our group came tripping over to my desk and told me that Mr. Hattori wanted to see me. Being called by Mr. Hattori was not unusual and so I casually walked over to his desk. But what he told me struck like lightning: "Prototype 12 number two disintegrated in midair at Yokosuka and the pilot was reported killed. Will you rush over to the Naval Aeronautical Establishment right away?" I felt as though all the blood had been drained out of my head.

The loss of an aircraft during a flight test is not a rare occurrence. Although we repeatedly conducted strength tests and wind tunnel tests so as to gather data which could be used to make proper corrections for problems which might occur during actual operations, nothing is absolute when human beings are involved and some problems are simply unpredictable. I had already experienced two such unforeseen problems during the Prototype 7 program. However, in both cases, the pilot was able to escape by using his parachute and landed safely. But this time the pilot had not escaped. What in the world caused such an accident? Returning to my desk, I reported the news only to my lead men for the time being. Everyone looked gloomy, but clearly it was too late to do anything about it now.

DID THE PARACHUTE OPEN?

Leaving my worried team leaders behind me, I rushed to Yokosuka by night train. I kept thinking, "Was it a pure accident or a defect in design?" More than that, it pained me to think of the deceased pilot. As I lay in bed in the sleeper car, sleep would not come. Some distance away, I could hear the sounds of a group of people, possibly a charter group, drinking and making merry. The noise of their party was horrible to my ears.

Now that the accident had occurred, I wanted to know everything in detail at the earliest possible moment. Six and one-half hours from Nagoya, twenty minutes from Ohfuna, after a short wait and a train change, I finally arrived at Taura where the Naval Establishment was located. After waiting impatiently for morning to arrive, I visited the office of the director of flight testing. Standing there in front of him, I was momentarily speechless. In the next instant, words unexpectedly came from my mouth, "I must apologize." Although it had not been established that the design was responsible for the accident, these words seemed to be the most appropriate.

Only after attending meetings from morning to afternoon, did I finally learn the entire story of the accident. The deceased pilot was Mr. Masumi Okuyama, a test pilot from the flight test division of the Aeronautical Establishment. On that day he was conducting dive tests to investigate the problems associated with the variable pitch mechanism of the constant speed propeller. This was considered to be a high priority, because if each propeller blade's angle of twist did not change sensitively, then the airplane could not perform efficiently during air battles where quick, snappy motions at a wide variety of speeds were required. Also, any imbalance would be a source of uncomfortable virbration for the pilot.

Mr. Okuyama, who tackled this problem, was a veteran test pilot with nearly 2,000 hours of flight time in trainers and fighters. First, he safely completed the test dive from 1,500 to 500 meters, and then he began to dive again from 1,500 meters at an angle of about fifty degrees. The tragedy occurred at that time. According to the report, as prepared by Lieutenant Commander Nakano, when Mr. Okuyama's airplane dove between 400 and 500 meters without any sign of pulling up, it made a loud roaring sound followed by a loud bang. Instantly, the wing detached from the body, and the engine and propeller began to fall as one unit while the remainder of the airplane fell to the ground in pieces. Mr. Okuyama separated from the airplane, and as his body fell, people silently prayed, "Please, parachute, open!" As the parachute opened, a feeling of relief spread, but it was short-lived. At about 300 to 400 meters, his body left the parachute and fell rapidly to the earth where it was ruthlessly smashed in the shallow waters near the beach. The empty parachute vainly landed nearby.

According to the witnesses' statements and the investigation of the parachute, Mr. Okuyama was semi-conscious in midair and may have been under the illusion that he was on the ground. It seemed he unconsciously released the locking mechanism of his parachute by moving his hands during the fall. If he had been completely unconscious during the fall, he might have been saved. I deeply regretted Mr. Okuyama's death.

The Accident Investigation Goes around the Clock

The meeting which started the investigation into the cause of the accident was opened in an atmosphere of sorrow. Mr. Sugimoto, the director of the flight test division, was acting as moderator and said, "We must discard any preconceptions and proceed cautiously, searching for the true cause and finding a remedy. Moreover, we have been ordered to complete the task as quickly as possible." After this and following Lt. Comdr. Nakano's firsthand account, the Naval Aeronautical Establishment flight test division's Mr. Matsudaira stood up. He had been in charge of the Prototype 12's vibration tests since January 1939. Mr. Matsudaira looked pale, as if he had not been able to sleep the previous night. He went straight to the point, recognized by everyone: the airplane had fluttered.

Flutter is a vibrational phenomenon which can include wing, tail, ailerons, elevators, and rudder. It occurs as a function of the airplane's speed and is somewhat similar to a flag flapping in the wind. If it occurs, the airplane vibrates severely and usually suffers a midair disintegration. Perhaps the following example will make flutter easier to understand. If you hold a piece of paper in your hand between your thumb and forefinger and blow gently, the paper floats in the air, but if you blow harder, the paper begins to flap. This is flutter. If you use stiffer paper, it will not flutter unless you blow harder.

A fighter aircraft, which attains a terrific speed during a dive while dogfighting, must have a strong, stiff wing as well as other stiff structural members to prevent flutter. In a sense, whether flutter can be prevented may decide the fate of a fighter's performance. At this investigation, everyone's suspicions first focused on flutter as the cause of the accident. This was natural, since the airplane had disintegrated in midair after it picked up speed in a dive.

However, Mr. Matsudaira made the following comment which denied such reasoning: "The airplane would not be in danger of fluttering until it reached a speed of over 1,000 km/hr, judging from the results of the tests conducted in the past. Besides, previous accidents caused by flutter show that if it started on the wing, only the wing would be destroyed; in the case of the tail, the tail and the aft end of the fuselage would be damaged. This was an absolutely unprecedented case of the entire airframe instantly shattering into pieces. Therefore, I don't think the cause of this midair disintegration is ordinary flutter." The discussion then shifted to the significantly different pitch angles of the three propeller blades found at the scene of the accident. It was natural to focus on this, since the forward section of the fuselage containing the engine had twisted off with a loud roaring sound while leaving no trace of a sudden, nose-up motion.

But, despite our efforts, we were unable to determine the exact cause of the accident; we could only ponder over Mr. Okuyama's death. In order to find the cause, we decided to make a fresh start. The Prototype 12 was grounded indefinitely and countermeasures were taken to prevent further such accidents from happening in the future. This was the only way to repay Mr. Okuyama. We all attended Mr. Okuyama's memorial service, which was held after the meeting, and with bowed heads we apologized to him in our hearts.

After that, I examined the remains of the number two prototype, which had been gathered and arranged in the hangar, and also the map of the wreckage showing the position of the parts when they hit the ground. I found it was difficult to accurately estimate the sequence of breakup judging from the condition of the remains and the way the parts were scattered; the airplane had been almost completely destroyed.

A careful examination revealed the mass balance weight, which was attached to the elevators, had been sheared off at the middle of its supporting arm and was missing. This weight was required to prevent the elevators from fluttering. On earlier airplanes, which could not fly as fast, such weights had not been needed. But as performance improved and speeds increased, the weights became necessary, and we first used them on the Type 96 fighter. Examining the remains of the number two prototype, we were unable to reach a definite conclusion concerning the significance of the missing weight.

It appeared progress would be slow in determining the cause of the accident, because the breakup sequence was unknown and the pilot's testimony was of course unavailable. It was pointed out that the surface of the wing spar was poorly machined, and, as the designer, I was embarrassed. We were required to provide necessary test specimens and data, although the investigation would be conducted by the Navy and we would not be directly involved.

About ten days later, since we had to submit some data, the company dispatched Mr. Sone to the Naval Aeronautical Establishment and requested that he be allowed to look at the remains of the airplane and see how the investigation was progressing. Incidentally, the name of the Naval Aeronautical Establishment had been changed on 1 April to the Naval Aeronautical Engineering Establishment. Mr. Sone reported that the investigation was continuing both day and night. As difficult a job as it was, the Navy found the cause of the accident early in April because of Mr. Matsudaira's investigative studies. We were surprised but really admired this accomplishment.

According to the Navy's report, the accident occurred as follows: "The mass balance weight, which was attached to the elevators, cracked and eventually fell off because of repeated shocks of landings and takeoffs. As a result, the elevators were in a condition in which they could flutter. After the airplane started to dive and as its speed increased, the elevators began to flutter and this induced vibration into the entire airframe; consequently, it is presumed the airframe disintegrated instantly."

When the elevators started to flutter, the aft portion of the fuselage started to vibrate vertically; simultaneously, there occurred a vertical bending vibration of the wing and a vertical oscillation of the engine. In addition, a pitching displacement of the airplane occurred. Because the airplane had gone through a very complicated motion, most experts assumed it would take a long time to complete precise experiments and calculations. In spite of this, Mr. Matsudaira reached his seemingly bold conclusion in a matter of weeks by using his uniquely sharp perception, theories, and a simple model.

But the majority of people involved still had their doubts that elevator flutter could have caused vibrations severe enough to tear the engine section from the airframe. In the end, however, Mr. Matsudaira's explanation was accepted, and the balance support was redesigned so as to make it stronger. Needless to say, an improvement to prevent malfunctioning of the constant speed propeller was also included in this redesign program. This was absolutely necessary in order to meet the dogfight performance requirements; and in fact the dive test in which the accident occurred had been part of the program to improve dogfight performance. Because of these remedies, no similar accident occurred. We had been painfully reminded that

THE CAUSE OF THE ACCIDENT IN WHICH
PILOT OKUYAMA WAS KILLED

In the number two prototype
aircraft, piloted by Mr. Okuyama,
the mass balance weight was
broken off of the elevator.

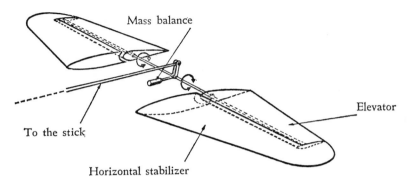

Mass balance

To the stick

Horizontal stabilizer

Elevator

With mass balance

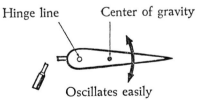

Mass balance   Center of gravity

Hinge line   Elevator

Does not oscillate easily

Without mass balance

Hinge line   Center of gravity

Oscillates easily

In the case of Mr. Okuyama's airplane, the elevator oscillation induced vibration in the airframe and caused the midair
disintegration.

the elevator mass balance was too important to be designed by "common sense" as opposed to rational analysis.

The tragedy of Mr. Okuyama's death occurred because we stepped into a technically unknown region which included high maximum speeds and constant speed propellers. In this sense, the accident could not have been avoided if we were going to achieve the performance levels demanded of the Prototype 12 fighter. But, as the designer in charge of this airplane, I felt very bad about the accident, just as I had told the flight test director on the day after it had occurred. I offered a silent prayer and told Mr. Okuyama that our aeronautical engineering gained a valuable milestone in experience because of his sacrifice.

The First Campaign

When the accident countermeasures were completed, rigorous testing programs were started by the Aeronautical Engineering Establishment's flight test division and Yokosuka Air Corps. In the middle of May 1940, we were officially informed that the Navy was sending the Prototype 12 to the front in China about the middle of July. Of course, we all thought, "finally, it's happening," but honestly speaking, we had a feeling of being behind schedule. Prior to the accident, our schedule had called for deployment by the end of April, based on the assumption that everything would go smoothly. It is understandable that Mr. Okuyama's accident would cause a delay of one or two months. Furthermore, we were sending these new prototypes very far away from home where there would be no spare equipment or engineers if something should go wrong. For the Prototype 12 to participate effectively in combat, it first had to perform its operational tests satisfactorily, and at the same time pilots must be trained. Modifications would also be necessary, based on our experiences during the tests.

The delay of nearly two months is understandable when one considers that our plans were made without allowing any cushion in the schedule. One day, I was sent to Yokosuka to make arrangements for spare parts, which were to be furnished by Mitsubishi for the operational tests. Looking at the Prototype 12 fighter flying around in the blue sky with the fresh markings of the rising sun painted on its fuseleage, and listening to the roaring sound, I keenly felt that this fighter was no longer in the hands of the company and its design team.

At the meeting where arrangements were made for the combat experiment, I was already on the listening end. The man in charge of testing at Yokosuka Air Corps was Lt. Mambeye Shimokawa, who had just recently reported for duty at the end of 1939. He served as the fighter divisional officer. We knew Lieutenant Shimokawa quite well because of his efforts to assist in the development of the Proto-type 12 during early design stages. It was he who had conducted many tests for the purpose of discovering the cause of the accident to the number two Prototype 12. Operational tests, based on actual combat experiences, were continued by the Navy pilots under the leadership of Lieutenant Shimokawa, his objective being to advance to the front lines during July.

As an example of the type of tests performed, firing tests of the cannons were conducted fifty or sixty times under various loading conditions such as steep banks or pull-ups. Finishing touches were made to the operational fighter by improving the gun support system in the airframe so as to assure failure-free operation of both the 20-mm cannons and the 7.7-mm machine guns in any flight attitude.

Under certain conditions, a phenomenon know as "vapor lock" occurred, in which the fuel supply to the engine was cut off. A high rate of vaporization takes place when fuel in an airplane's tanks is heated by the summer sun while on the ground and is subsequently subjected to low pressures at high altitudes without having adequate time to cool. However, research showed that this problem could be solved by using a special fuel which did not vaporize so easily. In addition to vapor lock, we had other things to worry about, such as the difficulty in releasing the external fuel tank at high speeds, and the overheating of the engine during a prolonged air battle. Thanks to the concentrated efforts of concerned personnel, we found a remedy or at least a partial solution to each problem, although our solutions were not always perfect!

I learned through the Navy bulletin that some Prototype 12s had finally been sent to China in July after the Navy was reasonably sure the airplane would be usable for actual combat operations. Thereafter, the state of affairs in China was sometimes revealed to the company, but only in the nature of requests for technical improvements required for the Prototype 12. Although I was busily working away on the design concept of the next airplane, the Prototype 14 fighter, I sometimes was curious to know about the Prototype 12 and would ask myself, "Is the Navy continuing the satisfactory operation of this aircraft in China?"

The Name "Zero Fighter" Is Born

A few days later, at the end of July 1940, the Prototype 12 carrier-based fighter was officially accepted by the Navy. It so happened, this was the Japanese year 2600. The airplane was named, "The Type Zero Carrier-Based Fighter, Model 11," taking the last digits of the 2600 for its name. "Zero fighter" was the abbreviation of the official name. A copy of the official acceptance decision was sent by the main office of Mitsubishi in Tokyo to the Nagoya plant, where it was circulated in the design room.

Since it was traditional for the military to use the last two digits of the current Japanese year in naming new aircraft, it was quite understandable that the Prototype 12 would be known as the "Type 00," or "Zero" for short. The change in name from Prototype 12 to Zero showed, in itself, the interval of three years required for the birth of the new fighter.[1] Actually, this was the normal length of time required in those days for the development of a single-engine fighter from its initial concept to the final form. I remember having a strange feeling toward the name Zero, different from what I had felt toward the names of some of my other designs.

Because I did not even dream of Japan becoming allied with Ger-

1. Translators' note: The twelfth year of the reign on the present emperor was Japanese year 2597, which corresponded to 1937 in the Western world.

many and engaging in war against the United States and England, I
never imagined that the Zero would be called "Zeke" by foreign
opponents or that it would march through history, first with glory
and then with tragedy.

THE FIRST VICTORY IS REPORTED

For some time after the new fighter was officially accepted, we did not
hear any reports of how it was faring in China. The first such report
finally came two months after the Zero's deployment to China on the
evening of 13 September 1940. Mr. Hattori, who was normally un-
perturbed, looked unusually happy and said something like, "Mr.
Horikoshi, it's big news!" He told me that Zero fighters had recorded
a major victory in China that day by destroying twenty-seven enemy
airplanes. The Navy Aeronautics Headquarters decided to give an
unprecedented commendation to Mitsubishi for the design and development of the Zero fighter and also to Nakajima Aircraft for the
design and manufacture of the Sakae engine which powered the Zero.
Dai-Nihon Heiki Company was also commended for the production
of the 20-mm cannons.

"Finally, they did it!"—that was our typical reaction at Mitsubishi.
Feelings were all the more strong because of the suddenness of the
news. Mr. Hattori told me that the commendation ceremony would
be held on 14 September and I should be present. I was stunned at
this speedy process: first victory and then a citation presentation,
all within two days. At the same time, I thought I understood how
happy the Navy really was. We hurriedly left that night for Tokyo,
and the next day I attended the ceremony held at the Ministry of the
Navy, standing behind the executives from Mitsubishi's main office
and the Nagoya aircraft plant. It was a hot day, although it was early
in fall. We were dressed in suits and ties, and as we walked into the
red-carpeted room, I saw some familar faces from other companies
and from the Navy. Wiping our sweaty faces with handkerchiefs,
we congratulated each other. The citation, which was announced at
the ceremony, read as follows:

A Search for a New Fighter

The Japanese Navy's Zero fighter (bottom), which was unrivaled during the early to mid portions of World War II, was created on the basis of the experiences of two other fighters we had previously designed, the Prototype 7 and the Type 96 carrier-based fighters, which are shown in the top and center photos respectively. Our design technology was unsophisticated when we designed the Prototype 7, and the completed airplane looked like a slow-witted duck as can be seen. But, as I gained experience and confidence as a fighter designer, my team eventually produced the Type 96, which in its day surpassed the level of the world's best fighters. This confidence would later support me during the seemingly impossible design of the Zero.

The Beginning of the Ordeal to Turn Impossibilities into Possibilities

The performance requirements demanded by the Navy for the Zero were so severe as to seem almost impossible. However, if we could achieve them, we would have the world's best fighter; encouraged by this thought, I exhausted myself in design work. In this photograph, I (on the right) am standing with my assistant, Mr. Yoshitoshi Sone. This picture was taken just prior to the beginning of the design of the Zero. Below is an aerial view of the Nagoya aircraft manufacturing plant of Mitsubishi Heavy Industries. Our design room was in the large, flat-topped building in the lower center.

Studies and More Studies

This picture shows some of the many volumes of calculations and reports that were produced during the design of the Zero. A one-eighth scale wooden wind tunnel model is shown below along with its drawing.

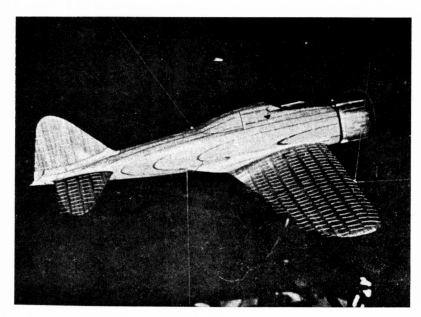

Successive Experiments, Tests, and Valuable Sacrifices

Along with design work, tests were performed using models and mock-ups, some of which are shown here. These pictures were buried under many documents for over twenty-five years. The top picture on the right shows the wind tunnel test model. Air came out of the circular cylinder at the right. The top left picture shows another wind tunnel test model used to study airflow. Below in the center is seen an experiment which determined the wing's natural frequency for flutter studies. Below right is shown the number 2 prototype undergoing vibration tests. In spite of the many tests, accidents claimed the lives of two of our precious pilots. The bottom picture on the left shows the remains of the number 2 prototype, which disintegrated in midair with the loss of its pilot. Through much difficult testing, the Zero was refined to become a fine young warrior.

CONSTANT SPEED PROPELLER
The Zero's engine was
able to operate at
full power at all times
because the propeller
blade angle automatically
changed as the aircraft's
speed varied from high to low.

7.7-MM MACHINE GUNS

CANO

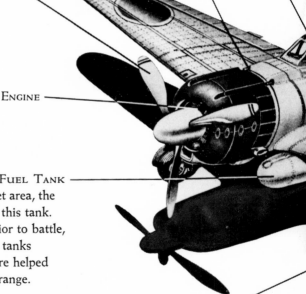

ENGINE

DETACHABLE AUXILIARY FUEL TANK
When heading to the target area, the
airplane burned fuel from this tank.
The tank was dropped prior to battle,
and fuel from the internal tanks
was then used. This feature helped
to give the Zero its great range.

RETRACTABLE LANDING GEAR
When the landing gear is exposed to the
airstream, there is a great deal of drag
which reduces high speed performance. We
used a retractable landing gear for the
first time on a Japanese fighter and it
helped to give the Zero incomparable
speed and range.

Features of the Completed Zero Fighter

The Zero finally materialized after we had gone through many hardships and sacrifices. The secret of its mysterious performance was in its carefully refined, lightweight airframe design as well as other features shown below. The airplane was later revised many times. The model shown here is the Type 11, which was the first Zero produced.

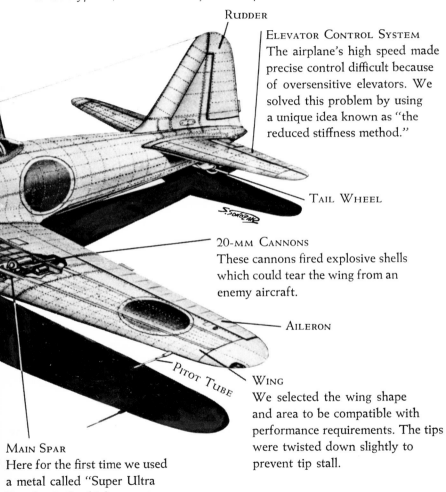

RUDDER

ELEVATOR CONTROL SYSTEM
The airplane's high speed made precise control difficult because of oversensitive elevators. We solved this problem by using a unique idea known as "the reduced stiffness method."

TAIL WHEEL

20-MM CANNONS
These cannons fired explosive shells which could tear the wing from an enemy aircraft.

AILERON

PITOT TUBE

WING
We selected the wing shape and area to be compatible with performance requirements. The tips were twisted down slightly to prevent tip stall.

MAIN SPAR
Here for the first time we used a metal called "Super Ultra Duralumin," which was stronger than previously used materials.

No Rival over the Pacific

As the Zeros were sent to the front lines, their uncanny ability to dogfight allowed them to defeat many enemy fighters. The four pictures shown above are of the major enemy fighters that confronted the Zero. They are, starting with the upper left and going clockwise, the F4U (USA), the F4F (USA), the Spitfire (England), and the F6F (USA).

Below are shown two different models of the Zero. The Zero fought almost alone against the new enemy fighters. The photo on the left shows the Zero model 21 at the beginning of the war. On the right is the Zero model 52 "Hei" of 1944. The engine cowl is different and more guns have been added in the wing. Because of the serious lack of both pilots and materials toward the end of the war which delayed the appearance of successor aircraft, the Zeros were forced to fight difficult battles, and one by one they disappeared in the skies of the south.

Mr. Kowshiro Shiba
President
Mitsubishi Heavy Industries Company Limited

Citation
On 13 September 1940, a group of "Type Zero Carrier Fighters" attacked and destroyed twenty-seven enemy fighters over Chungking. This was mostly due to the superior quality of the Type Zero carrier fighter, and we are very grateful for your endless efforts to accomplish this achievement.

14 September 1940
Teijiro Toyota
Vice Admiral and Chief
Naval Aeronautics Headquarters

As I was listening to the presentation of the citation, I could imagine Zero fighters over China taking an active role in the air battles. The victorious results of the battle were reported in the morning newspaper; under the headline "Imperial Navy Fighters Down Twenty-Seven Enemy Aircraft," the paper printed in detail how the battle was fought. However, there was no mention of the name Zero fighter or the name of the base from which the Zeros sortied. Also, the number of Japanese airplanes used during the battle remained a secret for reasons of security.

About this time, there was a wholesale arrest of foreign agents in Japan. We knew, of course, that the fighters mentioned in the article were the Zeros which had gone to war in July, but we could not learn anything else. We presumed the enemy airplanes were Russian-built I–15 and I–16 fighters, and our guess was substantiated by the article in the paper. Therefore, if we fought against the same number, we would easily win. But since we estimated the number of Zeros in China to be no more than thirteen or fourteen, it was certainly a big surprise to learn that twenty-seven enemy aircraft had been downed; this meant that the Zeros had been outnumbered more than two to one.

When we returned to the office, we found that everyone in the design room was discussing the news. I described the presentation ceremony, and we were all happy to learn of the glorious record of the airplane we had designed after much hard work. A few days later, I received a photostatic copy of the citation, made for me by the Mitsubishi management. It was still in my hands for a while after the war, although discolored by age. Everytime I looked at it, I vividly remembered the happy face of each individual as it was routed through our section.

Finally We Find a Challenge in the Sky

It was sometime after the end of the war when I finally received a detailed account of the battle for which we had received the citation, and it was far more successful than I had imagined. According to the report, Lt. Tamotsu Yokoyama from Omura Naval Air Corps and Lt. Saburo Shindo from Yokosuka Air Corps had been given special orders to go to the front, and flew to Hankow in late July, taking with them six and nine Zero fighters respectively. There they joined the Twelfth Air Corps based in Hankow. On 19 August 1940, twelve Zeros, led by Lieutenant Yokoyama, made the first attack on Chung-king, escorting fifty-four Army Type 96 bombers. Lieutenant Yoko-yama searched carefully for enemy fighters but could find none in the Chungking skies or even in the vicinity. It was so peaceful that there were even black hawks flying about. Lieutenant Yokoyama and his men returned to their base empty-handed but able to control their disappointment. On the following day, 20 August, twelve Zeros led by Lieutenant Shindo went into action, but they too had the same experience. It appeared the Chinese air force had discovered the new Japanese fighter and was avoiding it. Facing no challenging enemy was good news for our bombers, as it permitted them to operate more efficiently and accurately in bombing military targets. The invasion of Chungking by Zeros was particularly significant, since the round trip of 1,800 kilometers by a single-engine fighter was unprecedented in the history of the world's military operations. Already the Zero was exhibiting its extraordinary range, which could be found in no other aircraft.

On 12 September, twelve Zeros led by Lieutenant Yokoyama again invaded Chungking, escorting twenty-seven Army attack bombers. They penetrated deep into enemy territory as far as their fuel reserves would take them while searching for enemy aircraft, but again they returned fruitlessly. However, on that day some information was gathered that would stir up the pilots' fighting spirit. With the Zeros that day also flew a Type 98 land-based reconnaissance airplane which observed the Chungking area from a high altitude. By means of aerial photographs, it was learned that thirty-two fighters were on the ground. Based on the evidence from these pictures, along with other information, it was surmised that the Chinese fighters had fled behind the mountains shortly before the Japanese fighters arrived at Chungking, but now that the Japanese fighters had apparently left the area, the Chinese fighters returned, flew about randomly for a while, and eventually landed at their bases. Lieutenants Yokoyama and Shindo discussed the matter and came up with an idea. On the following day, they translated this idea into action.

THIRTEEN ZEROS DEFEAT TWENTY-SEVEN ENEMY AIRCRAFT

On 13 September, thirteen Zeros under the command of Lieutenant Shindo and Lieutenant Junior Grade Ayao Shirane invaded Chungking, escorting a company of Type 96 attack bombers. As before, the Zeros pulled above the bombers until the mission had been completed and then started back home, still escorting the bombers but remaining in the rear. On this day, however, their course of action was different from the previous missions. A Type 98 reconnaissance plane turned back and climbed to a high altitude over Chungking. As it was loitering in the clouds, its pilot saw many small dots approaching Chungking from the southwest. When Lieutenant Shindo received the reconnaissance plane's message, he too turned back toward Chungking along with his command of thirteen Zeros. Dropping down to a lower altitude, he led his planes to the north side of the city and there they waited while intensely watching the southern sky. Because his group was on the dark side of the city, and the enemy would be on the light side, he knew it should be easy to see the Chinese airplanes. Slowly, the Chinese fighters approached above the city; they did not notice the presence of the Zeros. Lieutenant Shindo quickly counted nine groups of three aircraft, comprising a formation of twenty-seven enemy fighters.

It was Lieutenant Shindo's intention to destroy every one of the Chinese fighters. First, he climbed to altitude and instructed his pilots to spread out, as if casting a net. Then, after warning his men not to fly too fast, he pulled the trigger of his 20-mm cannons as he headed for the first enemy fighter. His men found their own prey and each rushed at the target. The effectiveness of the 20-mm cannons was unbelievable; if the shells hit the wing root, they destroyed the entire wing. This is understandable if one remembers that the wing of an aircraft is under heavy load when it is going at high speed, and under such circumstances the wing will come off very easily when hit.

During the battle, the Japanese pilots could tell that the enemy aircraft were I–15 and I–16 fighters, which had also been seen in the Nanking district. Once the enemy formation had been broken up, the Chinese fighters went down one after the other while sending up thick, black clouds of smoke. Lieutenant Shindo made a steep climb and positioned himself away from the battle so as to observe the action. Below him, high speed Zeros surrounded the Chinese aircraft, and the I–15s and I–16s continued to go down. Zeros also caught and destroyed those which had temporarily managed to escape from the siege. One Chinese aircraft did escape to a lower altitude; it was chased, and as it dove, it went straight into the ground. After a while, there was not a single Chinese fighter anywhere to be found. I was told the entire operation took about ten minutes.

Design Technology Victory

When Lieutenant Shindo returned to his base and collected the combat reports, he found there had been a total of twenty-seven enemy airplanes shot down, including those which crashed while being chased and those destroyed after landing. In contrast, of our thirteen aircraft, one suffered a hit in the fuel tank and three received some other minor damage. Lieutenant Shindo commented that he did not think the battle's outcome was a miracle; to the contrary, he believed the victory was a result of the enemy's overconfidence and use of traditional tactics. Consequently, we were able to strike the first blow from the best position, and owing to these splendid advantages, as well as the Zero's speed, range, performance, and armament, which were vastly superior to those of the I–15 and I–16, success was ours. I could well understand the comment of one pilot who participated in this first aerial combat: "When we chase the enemy, we must be very careful not to get in front of him!" These words vividly described the superior speed and acceleration of the Zero. Because the Zero was so much faster than the Type 96, which was noted for its tight turning radius, the Zero was able to engage twice its own number of enemy aircraft, including those that had temporarily escaped from battle.

I was told there were reports of a malfunctioning of the external fuel tank release mechanism after the Zeros went into the attack position. This apparently forced some of our aircraft to go into battle with the tanks still attached, but even this did not cause a problem. The Zero, being lightweight and aerodynamically clean, and having only a few accessories, had no trouble fighting the I–16s, whose performance was not near the top international level.

The Naval Aeronautics Headquarters, after issuing the citation, decided to let Nakajima also produce Zeros. In this case, the question of manufacturing and patent rights was not an issue, as it might have been between private companies under other circumstances. All the Navy had to do was pay Mitsubishi an appropriate amount of money for the design of the aircraft and then instruct us to transfer all technical data and assistance to Nakajima. Toward the end of September 1940, a group of executives and engineers from the Koizumi plant of Nakajima, who had been instructed by the Navy, visited the Mitsubishi Nagoya plant. We offered all relevant data and conducted preliminary discussions to assist them in starting up production of Zeros. In September 1941, Nakajima finished and rolled out its first Zero fighter.

Now that the evaluation of the Zero was complete, I could think back to the time when the Navy had voiced its displeasure with this aircraft. Two years earlier, when the design of the Prototype 12 was under way, the characteristics of this all-purpose fighter were challenged by an influential frontline military organization. The Twelfth Air Corps had violently criticized the armament by saying, "20-mm cannons installed in the wing have only disadvantages and no advantages." This drastically affected the Navy's policy of fighter requirements, and until recently even our best flight test pilots appeared to be puzzled about the relative merits of different armaments and could not decide if cannons were more effective than machine guns.

As stated earlier, Lieutenant Shimokawa, who handled the entire operational tests of the Zero, arrived on the scene at Yokosuka Air Base just in time and succeeded in persuading the pilots to accept the 20-mm cannons. His efforts greatly helped to expedite the dispatch of Zeros to the front despite the accident to the number two aircraft. I thought Lieutenant Shimokawa must have been very happy when he learned of the Zero's first combat success.

If the opportunity presented itself, the Zero could record the same kind of victory every day. It was the kind of airplane that had the ability to exhibit remarkably superior characteristics if it had a place to perform actual operations. However, an airplane's value in combat cannot be determined simply by comparing performance figures. At the beginning of our planning for the Prototype 12, I stated something to the effect that "a fighter is an airplane which fights; it is not one which merely establishes performance records." Later, I wondered who might have read this statement and if they remembered it. On the other hand, I felt pain in my heart concerning the course of events in which the Zero was to be tested. Neighboring China had been the source of our own culture for about 2,000 years.

We Make Improvements One after the Other

After the first combat victory, the papers continued to report on the remarkable activities of the Zero. As usual, the name Zero did not appear. But for those of us involved in the project, it was clear that the term "Sea Hawks" meant Zeros, as for example the headline of the paper might read, "Our Sea Hawks' Great Success."

Meanwhile, at the Mitsubishi plant, we were continuing the production of Zeros and were delivering Model 11s each day. We could also imagine the importance of the Zero's activities at the front. Because the program had entered the production phase, my opportunities to visit the production plant decreased, but I still had occasions to go there, usually to supervise very minor design changes or modifications. Of course, we did not have a system such as an assembly line in those days. In the big plant, there were always four or five airplanes lined up; some were just airframe skeletons, while others were painted and ready to roll out. Assembly crews and groups, ranging in size from two up to as many as sixteen, were busily working. When a group completed its work on one aircraft, it moved to the next aircraft and repeated the same task. As I walked about, calling to the crew over the ear-splitting roar of the rivet guns, I was reminded that the Zero's record of accomplishment was due in large measure to these hard-working people here in the background who would never receive any glory. Through their efforts, the Zeros were produced at the rate of about one per day and were flown from Kagamigahara to Yokosuka.

Meanwhile, starting with aircraft number sixty-seven, both wing tips were redesigned so that they could be folded straight up at a distance of about one-half meter inboard of the tips; this made it easier to handle the airplane while on an aircraft carrier. These Zeros were known as model 21s. Thus, the designation A6M2a was assigned to the Model 11 and A6M2b to the model 21. I remember it was Mr. Hirotsugu Hirayama's idea to design this wing tip folding mechanism. In the Zero model 11 or model 21, the first digit refers to airframe revisions while the second refers to engine variations. A change from 11 to 21 shows there was a significant visible modification to the airframe, but the engine remained the same. We delivered a total of about 120 Zeros, including prototypes, to the Navy by the end of 1940.

The model 21 was about to undergo another modification very

soon. A small, winglike tab called a balance tab was added to the trailing edge of the ailerons starting with aircraft number 127. Its purpose was to ease the operation of the ailerons at high speeds, since pilots had complained about heavy aileron forces even with the prototype Zeros. This was understandable considering the fact that the Zero was an order of magnitude faster than previous Japanese fighters. Because of these complaints, which became louder as time went on, the Navy Aeronautical Engineering Establishment offered the suggestion of using balance tabs, and we quickly decided to accept the idea. Unfortunately, a Zero fitted with balance tabs would soon have an accident which would cost another precious life, but we could not foresee this occurrence at that time.

The Zero Exhibits Its Fighter Performance during the Army/Navy Contest

Since the Zero first tasted battle, its remarkable activities in China received much publicity in the papers. There also was to be an occasion at home when the Zero's performance could be demonstrated to its full extent. This was at the Army/Navy joint performance contest held in January 1941. A similar contest had been held each year since 1934, but had been discontinued when the demands of the Second Sino-Japanese War became too great.

The Army now proposed to the Navy's Yokosuka Air Base that a joint contest be held, consisting of dogfights, speed, climb performance, diving zoom performance, climb and turn performance, and other types of maneuvers. The three following types of airplanes would be entered by the Army:

1. A modified Army Type 97, noted for its dogfight performance.

2. The model 44, later known as the "Shoki," which was an attacker possessing good speed and climbing ability.

3. The model 43, later known as the "Hayabusa," which was a fighter with characteristics similar to those of the Zero.

The Navy accepted the proposal and decided to enter only one fighter, the Zero, to compete against the Army's three models. In the contest, the Zero would be handicapped, as might be expected, since the evaluation would not consider several of the Zero's strongest points: its ability to land on aircraft carriers, its ability to serve as a long-range escort, and its 20-mm cannons. In comparison to the Zero's all-around abilities, the Army's three airplanes were all specialized aircraft. They either were designed to excel in speed and climb performance or did not have an exceptionally long range. Therefore, for the Zero to compete in the specialized events with each of these Army aircraft, it naturally would face severe difficulties, but this was to be expected and a loss would not be a disgrace.

The results of the contest were unexpectedly good. On 10 February when I visited Yokosuka Air Corps, I heard about the splendid record established by the Zero from Lieutenant Shimokawa and others who participated in the contest. The Zero did not lose a single event except for the climb contest. The Army's model 44 proved to be superior in the climb, as it was specifically designed for high speed and climb and utilized a much more powerful engine than did the Zero. The Zero had good acceleration during dives and did not permit other airplanes to come close in the excess climbing performance contest; it was also better than the other three fighters in dogfight performance. In turning performance in a vertical plane, it was vastly superior to the others. Lieutenant Shimokawa commented, "If the comparisons had been made in all-around performance, including range and effectiveness of the 20-mm cannons, the superiority of the Zero would be even more obvious." This excellent record was established by an airplane which moved at the pilot's will, was aerodynamically refined, and possessed a unique control response. Lieutenant Shimokawa, among others, told me of the excellent results by saying, "Really, you designed a good airplane for us. Thanks to you the Navy can be very proud of this machine." As I listened to his comments, a broad grin must have spread over my face.

Favorite of the Entire Navy

The victorious results of the fighting on the continent and the record of performance in the contest with the Army fighters were immediately accepted by even the most stubborn Navy pilots. A year earlier, when the airplane was transferred to Yokosuka Air Corps, it was not popular, because it seemed more "slow-witted" than the Type 96, but now it became the entire Navy's favorite. The old saying goes, "Spare the rod and spoil the child." Actually, the Navy was the parent that did not spare the rod, but discovered good qualities in its child. Furthermore, as a result of later operational tests, all performance requirements, including those considered difficult or impossible at the planning stage, were found to be satisfied or exceeded. This success can be attributed to engine improvements, the utilization of the constant speed propeller, and the successful airframe design, which included many new ideas. Both Commander Genda and Commander Shibata, who had exchanged heated arguments across the table at the council of planning meeting, would be satisfied with the performance. Nevertheless, the Navy and the manufacturer quietly continued to improve the airplane before, at the beginning, and during the middle of the Pacific war, as the Zeros were on their way to achieve many victories.

A solution was sorely needed to prevent power loss during high altitude flight in thin air. About this time, the Sakae engine with a two-stage supercharger, which could change to a higher speed at high altitude, passed the Navy's tests; and the decision was immediately made to change the Zero's engine to this new type. We completed the redesign of the airframe for this purpose by March 1941. This was the first big model change since we changed the prototype's engine from the Zuisei to the Sakae in the number three airplane. With the new engine, the Zero would be known as the model 32 and was designated as the A6M3.

The Zero continued to be used in China until August 1941. But the newspaper reports of such activities became subject to stricter censorship that year as a result of the "Newspaper and Other Printing Restriction Ordinance" issued in January. The Second Sino-Japanese War was worsening steadily and internationally Japan was being driven into a corner. According to records made available at a later date, the total kills recorded by Zeros, from their introduction into combat in July 1940 until 31 August 1941, were 266 enemy aircraft confirmed and three probables. Two Zeros were destroyed by ground fire. There was not a single Zero lost to an enemy fighter in combat. The total number of Zeros sent to China at that time was about thirty.

Starting with the groups lead by Lieutenants Shindo and Shirane on 13 September 1940, followed by the group of Lieutenant Yokoyama on 4 October 1940, and prior to 26 May 1941, Zeros dispatched to China received five citations from the China district fleet commander.

AMERICA AND ENGLAND ARE STILL UNAWARE OF THE ZERO

From the limited news available in Japan, I learned that the Zero had gained air superiority in China, but at the same time I wanted to know the reaction of foreign countries, especially China, to this fighter. Although it had been one year since the Zero first entered combat, the response to its appearence by foreign countries was unbelievably scarce. The monthly American airplane magazine to which I subscribed was full of information concerning new American and European models but never carried a single line about the Zero.

I ended up without a satisfactory answer to this mystery, but after the war's end, I learned a fact which symbolically expressed the response to the presence of the Zero in China. In 1937, the government of China had invited Claire L. Chennault, a retired U.S. Army Air Corps officer, to come to China and rebuild the confused Chinese air force, which had been split by many different policies and leadership techniques instituted by a host of foreign military consultants. Because of his competent control techniques and strict regulations, Chennault accomplished a great deal and his influence became much stronger; he was eventually in charge of aerial strategy in the war with Japan. The Chinese air force, after Chennault's efforts, showed formidable power. In August and September of 1937, those of our bomber attack companies that ventured out without escort fighters suffered many losses. But this situation changed after the Type 96 fighters were introduced into combat; they completely destroyed the Chinese air force.

Chennault was originally a fighter pilot, and because he was able to understand the excellence of the Type 96 fighter, his tactics were to avoid combat if a Type 96 should appear. If this could not be done, he would fight only in areas where Chinese troops held the ground. By this means, and by retreating further inland beyond the range of the Type 96, the Chinese air force was able to rebuild temporarily. Chennault immediately reported in detail to the U.S. Army about the new, high performance, all metal Japanese monoplane fighter, but his report was ignored. Chennault was surprised beyond description when, for the first time, Zeros appeared over Szechwan flying about at will during August and September of 1940. Again he sent all the information he could obtain about the Zero to England, Australia, and the United States. In his reports, he gave an impartial evaluation of Japan's new fighter, including a warning that disaster would result if British and American fighters attempted to dogfight with this new Japanese aircraft. Again, the authorities ignored Chennault's reports. In their eyes, Japan was still a developing country, especially with respect to aircraft technology, since only a few years earlier her industry had been completely dependent on assistance from foreign countries. They sincerely believed that Japan was incapable of designing and manufacturing the high performance fighter described in Chennault's reports. Japan was able to keep the secret of the Zero until the shocking attack on Pearl Harbor and the Philippines at the beginning of the Pacific war. This secrecy was not just the result of the Navy's efforts to hide Japan's latest aircraft, but I believe it was mostly because of the shortsightedness of many high-ranking Allied officers.

The first Zero model 32, known as the A6M3, equipped with the two-stage supercharged Sakae 21 engine, started flight tests in June 1941. According to our calculations, the A6M3 would have 980 hp at 6,000 meters altitude and should have a maximum speed 40 km/hr faster than the A6M2, which was equipped with a Sakae 12 engine and had only 950 hp at 4,200 meters altitude. During flight tests, we were disappointed to learn that fuel consumption and engine weight were both significantly increased while the actual speed increase obtained was only about 10 km/hr. In the past, flight test results tended to show better performances than the calculated figures. Perhaps it was natural for us to expect that more power would be developed at high speed, because more air would be forced into the carburetor than would be if the airplane were sitting on the ground with its engine operating. But, to our disappointment, both top speed and rate of climb for the A6M3 were below expected values. Our errors were the result of insufficient studies of high altitude engine performance and an obsolete method of calculating speed.

While requests for performance improvements continued to be made, the engine power required to meet them became more and more difficult to find. Because of this, we became obsessed with power.

The Second Victim

THE DEATH OF LT. MANBEYE SHIMOKAWA

Victorious results were reported from the front lines in China, and the production of the Zero seemed to be on the right track. However, we had to endure another tragedy before the Zero would show its unrivaled performance over the Pacific Ocean and demonstrate its true potential. In April 1941, about a year after the death of Mr. Okuyama in the number two Zero, there was another accident.

France had already been defeated in the European war, which was now one and one-half years old, and violent air battles continued between England and Germany. The ground battles had moved from the Balkans to Northern Africa and, during this time, both fighting and nonfighting powers were actively engaged in diplomatic negotiations. In this gloomy interlude, the Navy Air Corps was continuing an intensive flight-training program both day and night, consisting of practice operations far more difficult than those encountered in actual combat.

It was during the afternoon of 17 April 1941 that I heard the news of the second accident. It was a greater shock than the loss of Mr. Okuyama, since this time the pilot was Lt. Manbeye Shimokawa, fighter division chief of the Yokosuka Air Corps, an officer whom I knew and respected.

Lieutenant Shimokawa held the confidence of many people, because of his spirit of responsibility and endless desire to study and improve himself. He had an outstanding technical knowledge which was linked with a strong fighting spirit. In addition to these qualities, he was sincere and generous. His colleagues called him by his nickname, "Manbeye-san," and his seniors showed him special respect by calling him "Shimokawa-kun" and not just "Shimokawa," even in his absence. In the beginning, there were many pilots who could not see the value of the Prototype 12 fighter, but Lieutenant Shimokawa had the insight to see the aircraft's potential and devoted himself to its development. Engineers on my staff also knew him quite well since the first days of flight tests. When I told them he was killed in the accident, everyone uttered in disbelief with one voice, "What? Mr. Shimokawa?"

THE AIRPLANE FELL IN THE SHAPE OF A CROSS

That night, three of us left Nagoya: Naokazu Yui and Hirotsugu Hirayama, who were in charge of manufacturing; and myself, in charge of design. Early the next day, we reported to the Naval Aeronautical Engineering Establishment to hear the accident report and attend the investigation meeting.

According to the report, circumstances which led to the accident were as follows: During the afternoon of 16 April, Lt. Junior Grade Yasushi Nikaido, first divisional officer of the carrier Kaga, was practicing loops and dives over the Naval airfield at Kisarazu, Chiba prefecture. He was flying the Zero Model 21 fitted with balance tabs which reduced aileron stick forces. When he performed the dazzling tight loop, he noticed much more significant wrinkles in the left wing skin than ever before. He next went into a loose loop and noticed almost no wrinkles. After that, he went into a tight loop and again noticed the presence of deep wrinkles in the left wing skin. For a moment, his mind was uneasy, but he continued with the scheduled flight training. Finally, he started a dive from an altitude of 3,500 meters at an angle of about 50 degrees, and when he reached 2,000 meters at a speed of 590 km/hr, the wrinkling of the left wing skin again became apparent. As he reached about 600 km/hr, raising the airplane's nose gently, without any warning a strong jolt hit the airframe; this caused his vision to become blurred and he fainted. Regaining consciousness with the help of his strong will, Lieutenant Nikaido found his airplane in level flight and he noticed, to his surprise, that both ailerons as well as portions of the upper left and right wing skins were gone. The pitot tube, which measured the airspeed and was located in the leading edge of the wing near the left wing tip, was also bent, and the airspeed indicator was stuck at about 300 km/hr. Using the remaining controls, Lieutenant Nikaido calmly nursed the crippled airplane back to Kisarazu airfield. The accident was immediately reported to the Naval Aeronautical Engineering Establishment and the Yokosuka Air Corps.

Lieutenant Shimokawa, who was the fighter divisional officer of the Yokosuka Air Corps, must have experienced a strong feeling of responsibility when he heard the news. There were two Zeros in the Yokosuka Air Corps' hangar at the time; one was fitted with balance tabs similar to those on Lieutenant Nikaido's airplane and had been returned from the carrier Kaga because of wrinkles on the skin of its wing. The Yokosuka Air Corps conducted an investigation of the problem using this aircraft but could not find any reason for the accident. Lieutenant Shimokawa must have thought the quickest way to solve the problem was to flight-test another airplane in exactly the same way as Lieutenant Nikaido had flown his Zero.

The next day, the morning of 17 April, first flying the Zero without balance tabs, Lieutenant Shimokawa dove from 3,800 meters altitude at an angle of about 50 degrees and started to pull up when he reached a speed of about 640 km/hr, leveling off at 1,200 meters altitude. He paid special attention to the wing outer skin but observed only small wrinkles. He had already flown the Zero in the performance contest held between Navy and Army fighters in January of that same year and was confident of the Zero's structural integrity, since he had previously achieved a speed of about 680 km/hr. He next took up the other Zero fitted with aileron tab balances which had been built about the same time as Lieutenant Nikaido's, and climbed into the sky while being observed by many people on the ground. The first test was diving from about 4,000 meters altitude at an angle of about 50 degrees, gradually pulling the nose up at about 2,000 meters and returning to level flight at about 1,500 meters altitude. This test was completed safely and ground observers heaved a sigh of relief.

Lieutenant Shimokawa had been instructed by his superior, Lieutenant Commander Yoshitomi, prior to flight, "If you notice any wrinkles, stop the test immediately." He was not the kind of man who would forget such an order.

During the second test, he dove again from about 4,000 meters at an angle of about 60 degrees. When it seemed he was starting to pull up at about 1,500 meters, a large white fragment, which looked like a sheet of paper, flew off from the left wing followed by a black object. Then, after the airplane turned its nose to the left in a diving attitude, it rolled over twice and went down into the sea. Lieutenant Shimokawa did not bail out but went down with the airplane.

According to observers, the tail came off in the air and the airplane resembled a cross as it fell. This time, the airplane remained fairly intact while falling, which was different from the midair distintegration of one year earlier. The ailerons and horizontal tail must have come off in the air and we could not find them. It was possible that after both ailerons came off, they struck the horizontal stabilizers, detaching them from the fuselage. The airframe, engine, and propeller plunged violently into the water as one solid mass and were destroyed upon impact. In particular, the fuselage was badly twisted out of shape. A section of the main spar, which ran through the fuselage, and the outer skin of the wing, along with parts of smaller sections, were stuck together in a lump. The left wing tip was detached, although it suffered the least amount of damage. We were told it was difficult to find any clue as to the sequence of destruction because of the condition of the remains.

What Was Wrong with the Balance Tabs?

At the conference, after the accident was described, we had a discussion session which focused on the fact that similar accidents had occurred on two different airplanes fitted with aileron balance tabs.

Because the balance tabs had been originally installed as the result of a suggestion from the Navy, it appeared the investigation had already made considerable progress within the Establishment, since they probably felt a sense of responsibility. As stated earlier, the tabs were small winglike surfaces attached to the trailing edge of the ailerons, and were designed to ease the operation of the ailerons by utilizing additional airloads. However, according to comments made by Navy representatives, while the balance tabs could appropriately reduce stick forces up to a certain speed, they could also cause a strong force that would push up the trailing edge of the aileron without any input from the pilot. It was possible that the excessive force thus produced could destroy the control system. Or could it be that an overload acted on the wing and aileron because of the large aileron angles obtainable at high speed when the balance tabs were fitted?

Another opinion was offered that the accident might have been caused by flutter. This pointed to a more complex flutter mechanism than had previously been experienced, based on the rearward shift of the aileron's center of gravity with the balance tabs installed. But this type of flutter was not expected to occur at speeds lower than 750 km/hr. Mr. Matsudaira and the officials at the Naval Aeronautical Engineering Establishment explained that they were fairly sure flutter was not the cause, since the aircraft's speed at the time of the accident was not more than 650 km/hr. Lieutenant Nikaido also testified, "I didn't feel any vibration." The Naval Aeronautical Engineering Establishment released the straightforward statement that it believed the accident resulted from a failure to recheck the stress calculations for the wing, aileron, and control system when balance tabs were fitted.

On that day, opinions were submitted from a variety of positions. As in the case of the first accident, Mitsubishi was not directly involved in the accident investigation. Instead, we waited with much interest for the findings of the Navy's accident investigation team, which was led by Mr. Matsudaira.

We three Mitsubishi people were able to get a look at the remains of Lieutenant Shimokawa's airplane after the meeting. The thirty-

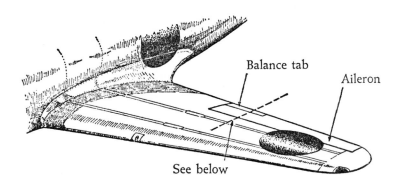

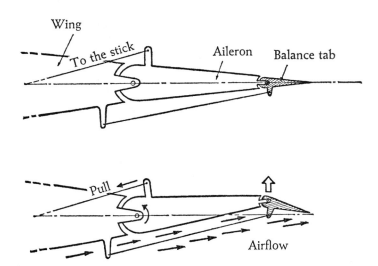

The balance tab helps the aileron to move more easily.

three-year life of this brave and promising officer was gone. For a while, we gazed at the ruthlessly deformed airframe in silence. It had not been so badly scattered as in the case of the first accident, but no matter how long we looked, we could not find a reason for the accident. We next decided to look at Lieutenant Nikaido's aircraft. It was in the same condition as described at the meeting. There was a gaping hole where the skin had pulled away, leaving the flush heads of the rivets protruding from the spar chord. These heads were quite small and did not seem to offer much resistance against pulling. We decided one improvement would be to increase the size of the countersinks in the spar chord so as to allow for a larger rivet head. While examining the wrinkles on the left wing, we found from the way they had formed that a twisting force had acted on the wing which pushed up on the leading edge and down on the trailing edge. Only a few wrinkles remained on the right wing.

That evening, we attended the funeral service for Lieutenant Shimokawa which was held at Yokosuka Air Base. He was promoted to Lieutenant Commander after his death. His funeral was in Shinto style. As I stood in front of his picture, I remembered him telling me the results of the performance contest against the Army fighters two months earlier. At that time he said, "You designed a good airplane for us. Thanks to you the Navy can be proud of this machine." And he shook my hand, smiling gently in a way that belied his strong personality. As I gazed at the lifelike picture of his happy face, I could not stop tears from coming to my eyes. This brave man, who had a strong sense of responsibility and a desire to learn, did not forget the orders of his commanding officer. Instead, his desire to discover the cause of the Nikaido incident must have caused him to try to bring the damaged airplane back to the ground. In so doing, he missed the opportunity to escape, and the fatal accident resulted.

Aeronautical Technology Progresses Rapidly

A month and a half later, on 13 June, a meeting of the accident investigation committee was held, and conclusions concerning the accident were reported by Mr. Matsudaira and others from the Navy. Mr. Sone and I represented Mitsubishi and we listened to the report. The cause of the accident was given as flutter, even though this had been described as an unlikely reason shortly after the accident occurred. I was very much interested in this conclusion and respected Mr. Matsudaira's diligence, since he had originally believed that flutter was not the cause but still investigated along those lines. He took a very close look at the remains of Lieutenant Shimokawa's Zero and at Lieutenant Nikaido's airplane. In particular, he examined the remaining wrinkles on the wing of Lieutenant Nikaido's Zero.

His reasoning was as follows: It had been reported that the skin of the wing wrinkled during the tight loop. A wing structure with wrinkled skin can easily be twisted because its torsional rigidity is greatly decreased. Consequently, a wrinkled wing will be subject to a dangerous torsional vibration at a speed much lower than an unwrinkled structure. The wrinkles left on the wing of Lieutenant Nikaido's airplane were localized and probably were there because the torsional resistance at that particular section was the weakest. This meant the amplitude of the wing torsional vibration was different from section to section, and the section with the most severe wrinkles should have vibrated the most. This realization startled Mr. Matsudaira. Had there been a serious shortcoming in the previous experimental models used to investigate the flutter problem? The flutter model, which was only a fraction of the size of the real airplane, had to simulate exactly all dynamic characteristics of the full-sized machine. In other words, the model wing must be made exactly similar to the real thing, including the distribution of stiffness, weight, and airloads in order to properly investigate flutter. However, the literature read by Mr. Matsudaira up to that time had only considered the exactness of wing shape and mass distribution and had not considered stiffness distribution. It was no wonder he did not get the correct solution the first time. This was a new concept for Mr. Matsudaira and for Japan as well.

While he arranged to get the new wing flutter model built, he conducted vibration and stiffness tests on the full-scale airplane. He took those results into account as he made the new model, and he made sure it had the identical vibration pattern of the real Zero. When a new flutter speed was calculated, it turned out to be barely 600 km/hr for a Zero fitted with aileron balance tabs. This was much lower than the previous 750 km/hr estimate. Without the balance tabs, the critical flutter speed was 630 km/hr. Consequently, Mr. Matsudaira frankly admitted his error and withdrew the comments he had made at the 18 April meeting.

In short, the state of the art of flutter technology in those days was obsolete when applied to the Zero, since it was a much faster airplane than its predecessors. The original estimate of critical flutter speed had been too optimistic. Because the manufacture of the airplane had been based on those optimistic estimates, a serious accident resulted. Now, only one and one-half months after the accident occurred, the cause had been found—an outstanding feat.

The flutter that had caused this accident was a complex vibration in which the torsional vibration of the wing and ailerons had coupled. In the course of the investigation, it became clear that this condition was more dangerous than one in which the wing and aileron vibrated together as a unit. The former condition was later named "Aileron Rotational-Wing Torsional Compound Flutter." It was also found that the much discussed aileron balance tabs acted to lower the flutter speed. As a remedy, the thickness of the outer wing skin was increased; the torsional strength was also increased by connecting stiffeners, known as longitudinal stringers; and, finally, a mass balance was added to the opposite side of the balance tab. The maximum dive speed of the aircraft was also temporarily reduced to 670 km/hr.

Thus, flutter technology was drastically altered as a result of this accident. The Navy lowered the maximum speed of all its aircraft based on the results of vibration tests of full-scale airplanes and wind tunnel testing of models. Test results were also reported to the Army aeronautical laboratories where the new technology contributed greatly to the advancement of aeronautical technology in Japan. In subsequent years, the Zero had no similar accident; the modifications made to prevent flutter had gained it another level of reliability.

Commander Shimokawa's death touched the hearts of those people involved in the project. At that time, Japan was already near a state of war, and the use of copper by the general public was prohibited except for a few accomplished sculptors who were allowed to use a limited amount. A bust of Commander Shimokawa was made from what little copper was available and placed in the Yokosuka Naval Air Base shrine, which was dedicated to the victims of naval air operations. There was a hill with a steep slope where pine trees grew at the south end of the air base; at the top of the hill was the shrine. Whenever I visited Yokosuka, I thought of Commander Shimokawa as I looked up the hill. Thirty years had passed since the founding of the Naval Air Corps and there had not been a single person who had received such outstanding honors as Commander Shimokawa, nor would there ever be.

No Enemy Rival
over the Pacific

WE CAN FIGHT IF WE HAVE ZEROS

On 22 June 1941, Germany renounced her nonaggression pact with Russia and declared war, thus beginning the invasion of the USSR. I happened to be at home that day, since my second son, one year and eight months old, had a fever. During the doctor's visit, I went out to buy a newspaper, which reported the event. I was shocked. Nazi Germany and Russia could not be compatible forever, but was the situation so acute as to require an attack on Russia? Since it was reported that America and England had immediately issued a statement declaring support for Russia, I thought Nazi Germany would surely follow the footsteps of Germany during the First World War. The future of Nazi Germany was gloomy and I could not help but think it was a risky gamble for Japan to be aligned with the Germans. Our doctor had a serious look on his face as he said, "Your son will be fine soon but the symptoms of Germany are very dangerous, aren't they?" Then, he left.

At the end of July, after negotiating with the provisional government of France, the Japanese military started to occupy southern French Indo-China. This was to shut off the material supply route to mainland China and, at the same time, secure the supply of raw materials for Japan. As a means of retaliation for this action, the United States broke economic ties with Japan; England and the Netherlands followed suit. Japan, which depended upon imported raw materials such as oil and bauxite from these three nations, was being strangled. Particularly for the aircraft industry, oil was crucial, being the raw material used to produce fuel, while bauxite was essential for the production of aluminum alloy from which the airframes were manufactured. The situation was such that within the Army and Navy serious consideration was now given to the possibility of war against the United States, Great Britain, and the Netherlands. Shortly before this time, the tone of articles in the newspapers began to reflect the bad feelings we had toward those countries as well as China. The general public was taking a militant attitude toward the actions of other nations and I thought this was a dangerous trend. Under these critical conditions, I was working hard both physically and mentally. Often I found myself completely exhausted, and the strain of the past year's overload was beginning to tell. During this time, I was involved in finishing the study concerning Commander Shimokawa's accident and also was making detail modifications to solve problems with the Zero which were coming in one after the other. We also had just started the design work for the Prototype 14, and finally, in September, my health became so bad that my doctor recommended I take a rest.

It was not only I who was affected by the overload. My right-hand man, Mr. Sone, was also ordered to take a month's rest. My rest period was put off until the basic design of the Prototype 14, "Raiden," was complete. I finished the structural drawings for the components, and when we reached the point where only production drawings were still to be done, I decided to let someone else carry out this task. If I kept on working and became worse, I would be causing much trouble for the company and the Navy. Realizing this, I decided to ask for leave. Mr. Hattori made the arrangements, and Mr. Mijiro Takahashi, who was two years my junior and had been a lead designer on the Prototype 10 carrier-based attacker, agreed to act as chief designer. He had recently returned from a visit to the Heinkel factory in Germany.

In the early part of September, I finished the necessary procedures to hand over my duties, and when Mr. Sone returned, I was allowed to leave. I spent the month of October very quietly at my birthplace in Gunma prefecture where my mother still lived. I would often go for walks and slept like a log at night. The hometown scenery was beautiful. When I went on a hike from Kozu ranch, which was on the border of Shinshu, to Karuizawa I could see leaves already taking on the scarlet colors of autumn, here and there, high above the ground. Days went by and I felt as though my work at Mitsubishi and the tense international situation belonged to another world.

However, the radio and the newspapers were reporting that Japan was slowly being pushed into a state of emergency. On 16 October, the cabinet of Prince Konoye, which had been engaged in difficult negotiations to break the deadlock with the United States, resigned. A new administration was put in power headed by Army minister Hideki Tojo. Listening to this news with my aged mother, I said to myself, "Finally, it looks as though we can't avoid war."

At the end of October, I returned to my home in Nagoya and felt as if I had returned to the atmosphere of my job, although I still remained at home. But I could not help thinking about work. While I was loafing at home, thinking about my job, the morning of 8 December 1941 arrived.[1]

From Disorientation to the Inspiration of Victory

"The Imperial Army and Navy have declared war against the United States and England in the western Pacific early in the morning of the eighth." At 6:00 A.M. on 8 December 1941, this special radio broadcast, which disturbed my early morning dreams, surprised everyone. At first, I thought it could not be true. But when I later heard His Majesty's grave tones, "with God's help . . .," I realized that things were very serious indeed. As one of His Majesty's subjects, I experienced feelings of tension and uneasiness. I was always aware of the geographic advantage, wealth, and strength of the United States, plus the outstanding advantages of industrial strength and aircraft

1. Translators' note: Owing to Japan's location with respect to the international dateline, Japanese time is one day later than that of the United States; hence 7 December in the United States is 8 December in Japan.

technology which she possessed. Also, since I was in the position of helping to produce airplanes that would fight against the United States, I thought immediately of the overwhelming differences in military strength between Japan and her opponents; logistically, to secure sources of raw materials, we would have to capture and occupy certain areas. As I considered these factors, I came up with a pessimistic forecast: the longer the war lasted, the less favorable were our chances to win. But the dice were cast! I thought the fighting would start in the west and South Pacific between the two navies and land, air, and sea battles would be fought near the Malaya Peninsula, in Singapore, and in the vicinity of the Philippines.

The Navy Air Corps planned to use a combination of Zeros, carrier-based attackers, and carrier-based bombers as well as a team of land-based Zeros and other attackers as their main strike force. But they did not expect a one-sided victory as had been achieved in China. America and England were proud of their advanced industrial status, especially in aeronautics.

By this time, about 520 Zeros, mainly the model 21, had been delivered to the Navy, but only 350 to 360 were ready for immediate mobilization, excluding those stationed on the Chinese continent, stationed at home, or undergoing repair. If these airplanes were to be dispatched to the site of battle, only a small number could be operational in each location. According to what Navy pilots told me, at the beginning of the war a single Zero was able to face from two to five enemy fighters successfully, and this philosophy was shown in the ratio of fighters we deployed on the carriers. However, attackers and bombers could not be deployed in the same way. My intuition was that after two to three missions, a large number of bombers would no longer be available for operations.

As if to allay my uneasiness, the newspapers and radio began to report great victories. The primary events reported were the attacks on Pearl Harbor and the Philippines. Newspaper headlines spoke of "Brilliant Victories in Hawaii and the Philippines," and the articles went on to say that the United States Navy had received a fatal blow during these two attacks. Much to my surprise, however, I heard no reports about the fighting ability of the Zeros.

Since the victories were so great, I was sure Zeros were actively involved, but I could not do anything but imagine. After the war, many details of the Pearl Harbor attack and the fighting record of the Zeros were made available, and the story is now well known. Briefly stated, at dawn Hawaii time on 7 December, about 353 airplanes including Zeros, Type 99 bombers, and Type 97 attackers took off from six carriers and destroyed the United States main Pacific fleet except for the aircraft carriers. About 230 military aircraft were also destroyed, but the fact that not a single aircraft carrier was in port left a shadow of disaster for us to face in the future. Japan's losses in this operation were nine Zeros, fifteen Type 99 bombers, five Type 97 attackers, and fifty-five crew members.

In reference to the Pearl Harbor attack and the effectiveness of the Zero, David A. Anderton, the famous American aviation reporter, wrote in the April 1949 issue of *Air Trails* magazine, "Through the angry skies over Pearl Harbor blazed tiny fighters, long, sleek and silvery gray. No recognition expert could have named them; their shapes were new and strange. On that day, the Japanese served notice to the world that they had abandoned their antique biplanes and angular monoplanes. Moving in complete secrecy, they had designed, built and used a striking force of one of the sweetest airplanes of all time. Those little fighters were the aces in the sleeve, the rabbits in the hat, and the cats in the bag. They were Mitsubishis, Type 00, the biggest mystery ship of the Second World War."

THE P–40 AND P–36 ARE OUTCLASSED

The Pearl Harbor attack was successful in general, but the Zero fighters did nothing more than down a few obsolete fighters with clearly inferior performance capabilities and destroy a number of parked aircraft. Pearl Harbor cannot be regarded as a battle in which Zeros fully exercised their potential. Rather, it was in the Philippines where Zeros first demonstrated their advantages to the world. It was about 830 kilometers between the Japanese naval base in southern Taiwan and the two major American air bases, Clark field on Luzon and Iba on the west coast of the island. Nichols field, in the suburbs of Manila, was 930 kilometers from Taiwan. The course was mainly over the ocean. Initially, attacks on Clark field and Iba were considered to be out of the question, since these bases were beyond the range of escort fighters. In addition, any action had to be withheld until after the Pearl Harbor attack, which meant that American aircraft in the Philippines would be anxiously awaiting the Zeros after receiving news of Pearl Harbor, and there might be difficult dogfights. Unless the Zero's range performance could be increased, there was danger of losing both the aircraft and its pilot during the return flight even if bombing attacks were successful. In other words, the success of this operation depended on the performance of the Zero fighter.

Without the Zero and its extremely long range, the operation would have been impossible. The distance between Taiwan and the Philippines was so great that the Navy originally prepared three small carriers to launch the Zeros in spite of its confidence in the aircraft. Eventually, the idea of using carriers was abandoned and engine specialists were dispatched from the Naval Aeronautical Engineering Establishment in an attempt to extend the cruising time of the Zero. Using the extended range fuel tank, these men were able to give the Zero a cruising time in excess of six hours, while still providing full military power capability for over thirty minutes while in enemy airspace. Thus, on 10 December (U.S. time) a fleet of Zeros took off from bases at Tainan and Kaohsung and reached the skies of the enemy bases by flying 830 kilometers nonstop.

Now, the biggest part of Luzon was under the control of the Zero. Army bombers were escorted by Zeros commanded by Lieutenant Shingo and Lieutenant Yokoyama. These aircraft attacked Clark field and Iba, destroying almost all the P–40 fighters and B–17 bombers they were able to find. P–36 and P–40 fighters attempted to dogfight with Zeros. I had been aware of these fighters since before the war but never considered them to be important rivals. They were heavier than the Zero and excelled only in dive speed. Their maximum speed was about the same as the Zero, but in all other aspects of performance they were inferior. Quite a clear difference could be seen during the dogfights. If, for example, an American airplane tried to escape by performing a dive, the Zero could usually get on its tail and attack, since the Zero could turn in a much tighter radius than either the P–36 or P–40. Also, at that time, most P–36 and P–40 aircraft were not fitted with self-sealing tanks and were protected only by steel plates which were easily destroyed by the Zero's powerful cannons. In fact, according to a statement released by the United States, about sixty airplanes, which constituted more than one-third of the total number of American Army aircraft stationed in the Philippines, were destroyed partially or totally during the first operation. Japan paid the price of losing three Zeros. It was reported that on the next day the Americans conducted an extended patrol in order to search out and destroy the Japanese carriers. They must have thought the Zeros took off from carriers in nearby waters; apparently it was impossible for them to imagine that Zeros had sortied from bases in Taiwan and had flown the 830 kilometers nonstop. Also on 10 December, thirty-four Zero fighters led by Lieutenant Yokoyama demonstrated their prowess over Nichols field. They fought dogfights against P–40s and P–36s and, although outnumbered about two to one, downed forty-four American fighters in forty minutes with the loss of only one Zero. P–40s and P–36s were simply no rivals for the Zero, even if we were outnumbered two or three to one.

There was yet another noteworthy record for the Zero that day. A flight commanded by Saburo Sakai of the Tainan Air Corps found a B–17 flying at about 8,000 meters altitude off the coast of Vigan on the west coast of Luzon, and downed it by concentrated fire of the 20-mm cannons. Being cautious, Flight Petty Officer Sakai reported this as an unconfirmed kill, but according to records made public by the United States after the war, this was the first B–17 to be lost in the Pacific theater.[2] The B–17 was the United States' big bomber and was nicknamed the Flying Fortress; it had an estimated range of about 1,400 kilometers, self-sealing fuel tanks, and defensive fire-

2. Translators' note: In the Japanese edition of this book, it was stated that Petty Officer Sakai's kill was the first B-17 shot down in either the European or Pacific theaters. We believe this is incorrect and have revised the English-language edition accordingly.

arms with only a small blind angle. Using its large payload as a weapon, the B–17 continued its brave actions and was the United States' only hope as she faced the Naval Corps of Japan lead by the Zero. But starting with Petty Officer Sakai's downing of a B–17, skillful Zero pilots downed a considerable number of them. The favored technique was to approach in the narrow blind angle of the B–17's defensive firearms and then fire at the pilot or the fuel tanks. Sometimes large numbers of Zeros would surround a B–17 and cause considerable damage by concentrated firing.

During the Philippine campaign, Zeros demonstrated their incomparable performance, easily downing enemy fighters and bombers. At the same time, they revealed to the world a glimpse of their extremely long range as had first been shown in China in 1940 when they flew a round trip over water in excess of 1,860 kilometers.

IF YOU ENCOUNTER A ZERO, FLY AWAY

Following these two triumphs, on 11 December victories at sea off Malaya were reported. Eighty-five airplanes of the Army attack corps took off from their bases in southern French Indo-China and attacked and sank the British cruiser *Repulse* and the new *Prince of Wales*. This action demonstrated a valuable lesson about battles fought between ships and aircraft: the British fleet was defeated because it did not have one single fighter in the air for protection. Apparently Japan failed to learn from this, since the very next day we followed in the exact footsteps of the British navy when we fought the Battle of Wake Island. The Wake Island invasion fleet consisted of light cruisers and destroyers; it suffered a fatal defeat, losing one destroyer and one cruiser and receiving damage to others. Only four U.S. fighters, Grumman F4F Wildcats, participated in this action! Later, Wake Island was eventually controlled by carrier-based attackers and Zero fighters dispatched from the Japanese fleet on the way home from Pearl Harbor.

The Grumman F4F had characteristics quite similar to those of the Zero, and I considered it to be the immediate threat to the Zero.

According to performance figures, the F4F had more power and a slightly greater diving speed than the Zero. It was the most important fighter being produced by the United States at that time. But we had confidence that we could defeat the F4F when we considered the Zero's overall performance, especially its firepower. According to our pilots' experiences, the Zero was superior in all phases of performance and could operate well at all altitudes. Zeros could always win against the same number of enemy aircraft, and usually the enemy would have to outnumber the Zero by two or three to one before the battle was a draw or even close. This was why American pilots thought the Zero had some sort of mysterious performance ability. Later, when the Zero had more opportunity to face the F4F, it was rumored that F4F pilots had orders saying, "You may retreat when you face a lightning storm or a Zero. Do not attempt to fight the Zero one to one."

Following the defeat of the F4Fs at Wake Island by Zeros, Japan gained air supremacy. But the Navy's valuable lesson—to protect ships with fighters—which should have been driven home, seemed to fade away in light of the reports of victory. It seemed as if everyone was caught up in the excitement of the moment and was freed from the shadow of doubts by continuous reports of victories. As my health had somewhat improved, I started back to work irregularly during December 1941. At the plant, the atmosphere was filled with earnestness, which seemed suitable since it was the factory where the victory-achieving airplanes were produced. Each employee was enthusiastic, realizing that the airplane he was working on would take an active role in combat within a few days. The number of people working at the plant had increased since the beginning of the war and we were producing, on the average, two Zeros per day. The one-sided battles fought with the Allied powers were also the subject of conversation in the design room. Early in the war, careful thinking led us to believe it was too soon to relax; we surmised that our victories must have been the result of temporary inactivity on the part of the United States Pacific fleet caused by the blow it suffered at Pearl Harbor. We believed Japan was able to enjoy the initial victories only because "while the cat is away, the mice will play."

However, as the successful operations in the Philippines, Indo-China, and Malaya were carried out with lightning speed, the optimistic mood started to fill even the designers' minds. I was beginning to feel we might be able to win as I saw one victory after the other; I had not anticipated that Japan could fight so well, and I also expected much stronger resistance from the United States and England. I continued to believe that Japan would be defeated if the war lasted a long time, but if we could end it fairly soon, I thought we could hold our losses to a minimum.

Shortly after returning to work, I had to take some additional leave because of severe pains in my back and chest which were the result of my doctor's rough examination. This time, with my family's approval, I took rest at a relative's home in Kamakura from about the end of 1941 until late February 1942. By staying at Kamakura, I felt I could closely follow the war action as well as the production and testing of airplanes, since it was close to both Tokyo and Yokosuka. The weather was warmer than in Nagoya and I spent each day doing the same thing, walking during the day and sleeping deeply at night just as I had done in November when staying at my hometown. I could not help but think about my work because of the war, but I tried to push away these thoughts by telling myself I must get well first.

During this period, a friend brought me a copy of *Taiyo* magazine which contained an interesting article. The magazine reported that Adm. Sankichi Takahashi, the former commander in chief of the Japanese Combined Fleet, stated that the Zero fighters developed by Mitsubishi were the reason for Japan's victories and that the Type 96, in his opinion, had also surpassed contemporary American, British, and Russian fighters. He also believed our aircraft technology was comparable to that of the leading countries.

ZEROS DOWN FIFTY WITH A LOSS OF THREE

While I was spending my leave in Kamakura, Zeros kept on winning. Since the successful occupation of the Philippines skillfully led by

Zeros, Army and Navy troops had moved farther south and established bases. The Navy Air Corps was no exception. Twenty-four Zeros belonging to the Tainan Air Corps advanced to the Jolo Island base in the Sulu Archipelago, southwest of the Philippines, by flying a distance of 2,200 kilometers. This was a difficult task, unprecedented for a single-engine, single-seat aircraft.

Japanese forces continued to sweep away anything which stood in the way. In January 1942 they landed in New Britain and New Ireland in the Solomon Islands and in February occupied Borneo. On 3 February, above the island of Java, a major dogfight took place, the first in many days since the invasion of the Philippines. Some sixty Zeros, which had flown 840 kilometers across the ocean on this mission, fought nearly one hundred enemy P–40s, P–36s, and Brewster Buffalos, downing fifty enemy aircraft while losing only three Zeros. The performance of the Brewster Buffalo was about the same as that of the P–40 and P–36; it was an easy opponent for the Zero.

By the end of the Java operation in early March, the Navy's South Pacific Air Corps recorded the destruction of 565 enemy aircraft, of which 471 were destroyed by Zeros. In Japan each day the radio reported victory after victory accompanied by the stirring music of the Navy march. Premier Tojo continued to repeat his familiar message, "It gives me great pleasure to report our imperial troops are winning everywhere, everytime they fight."

However, as the war intensified, the supply of necessities was clearly becoming shorter. As I finished my recuperation period in Kamakura and started back to work in the middle of February, steam for heating the office had been cut off and the quality of even our paper was visibly lower. In the center of the design room a wood stove was burning, but in the assembly plant, where rivet guns were hammering away, there was no heat at all and the airplanes were being assembled on the cold concrete floor. As far as design work was concerned, the production drawings of the Raiden had progressed to a state of near completion thanks to the efforts of Mr. Takahashi. The number one prototype of the Raiden would be complete by the end of February and was scheduled for flight testing in March. I left most of the work on this airplane to Mr. Takahashi and Mr. Sone, and acted as a consultant to them. This was because I was getting ready to investigate the design of the Prototype 17 "Reppu" which would be the immediate successor to the Zero. I planned to begin the design of the Reppu in the middle of April 1942.

This Is like Training

The Zero's accomplishments during the first part of the Pacific war were probably its most spectacular as compared to other times. I cannot list all of them here, but offer the following as an example. During the Indian Ocean campaign, Zeros fought the British Spitfires and Hurricanes. The Hurricane was slightly obsolete, but the Spitfire was Britain's primary fighter and was designed with the same emphasis on maneuverability as was the Zero, even though this meant sacrificing top speed. The Spitfire proved this concept was correct by establishing a two-to-one kill ratio while defeating Messerschmitt Me-109 fighters and other German aircraft during the Battle of Britain. The Zero and Spitfire had comparable dogfight performance, but the Spitfire was faster because it was fitted with a 50 percent more powerful, liquid-cooled engine. On the other hand, the Zero possessed extremely long range and, unlike the Spitfire, could be used as an escort. When the two aircraft met in combat, however, the Zero triumphed, since it could turn in a much tighter radius than the famous short turn of the Spitfire and also was much lighter. In one instance, in the skies over Colombo, thirty-six Zeros fought against scores of Hurricanes and Spitfires and downed seventeen Spitfires and twenty-one Hurricanes with a loss of just one Zero. Starting with this action, during the ten days of the Indian Ocean campaign, the Zero enjoyed fame as being the king of the skies against the British fighters. The pilots even said, "This is like training." Once they got into a dogfight, the difference in performance was very great and to the Zero's advantage.

The number of enemy aircraft destroyed or damaged by the Zero was nearly two-thirds of the total number destroyed or damaged by Japan. Many triumphs were attributed to the Zero when bombers or torpedo bombers completed their missions after Zeros had taken control of the airspace. This was why it was said that more than half of our victories in the air, on land, or on water should be credited to the Zero fighter during the early stages of the Pacific war.

At the time, I supposed the Zero was fighting as the heart of the Navy's airpower, but I did not think it really deserved all the praise it was getting. When I heard the praise still being given to the Zero later on in the war, I was surprised and very happy. It was understandable that the general public did not know much about the Zero, since we designers could not learn a great deal about it at that time either. Rather, it seemed the enemy had more knowledge of the characteristics of our new fighter than did our people. In fact, not only did the enemy military know about it, but it appeared the information had filtered into every corner of enemy society. As an example, I want to present briefly the statement made by Mr. Ichiro Hattori, then president of the Mitsubishi Trading Company:

> Immediately after the start of the Pacific war, some 3,000 Japanese scattered in Australia, New Zealand, and Java were sent to three district camps in Australia. In those days, the Australian Air Force was powerless against the Zero, which was increasingly exercising its power as the days went by. Every day in Parliament, speeches were made which criticized the Australian Air Force, and the newspapers even commented, "the country would be better off without such an incompetent Air Force." Because internees were allowed to read the newspapers, they were able to gain some knowledge of the war's developments. Among these articles, those concerning the Zero were of the utmost encouragement to the internees. Especially, four employees of the Mitsubishi Trading Company were unexpectedly well received because of the Zero and they were quite proud to be a part of the company which produced it.

Even the camp officers treated them with much respect, commenting: "You are employees of Mitsubishi, which is producing the Zero fighter." The officers based their praise merely on the name Mitsubishi without distinguishing between Mitsubishi Trading Company and Mitsubishi Heavy Industries. They received the Mitsubishi men courteously as if to say, "You accomplished a magnificent achievement even though you are our enemy." It was reported the Australians showed no sign of any retaliatory hatred. This warm feeling continued until August 1942 when the internees returned to Japan. On board the ship, they still received good treatment. They were allowed in the cabin, where normally a branch manager was seldom permitted, and enjoyed a pleasant voyage home. They were fed delicacies and slept in comfortable beds, but felt quite guilty when they thought of the others who had no choice but to eat unappetizing food and sleep in hammocks in the ship's hold. These four Mitsubishi employees appreciated the Zero all the way home to Japan and, at the same time, were grateful for the Australians' generous attitude.

I understand that after hearing about this, my superior, Mr. Jyoji Hattori, was deeply touched and reported the incident in detail to the executives of Mitsubishi Heavy Industries. Mr. Hattori wrote of this a few years later after Mr. Masatake Okumiya and I published a book about the Zero fighter.[3] He also told of another incident which I will repeat here. After the war, a Japanese woman who had read our book and was well informed about America visited Mr. Hattori and told him the following: "Immediately after the war, in American novels and magazines which I read, I occasionally came across sentences such as, 'It is easier to sweet talk a young woman than it is to shoot down a Zero,' or, 'That girl is tougher than a Zero,' and I didn't know what they meant until now. But, I was happy to learn that Zero was the name of the Japanese fighter designed by Mr. Horikoshi." I think this illustrates that the name Zero was better known outside of Japan than it was at home.

WE EXPERIENCE OUR FIRST AIR RAID

In the winter of 1942, while most Japanese were increasingly confident of victory, I was totally engaged in the design of the Reppu,

3. Translators' note: The English-language edition of this book was published in 1956 under the title *Zero!*, by Masatake Okumiya and Jiro Horikoshi, with Martin Caidin (New York, Dutton). It focuses on the combat history of the airplane.

which was to be the successor to the Zero. During the design, I thought that unless we used an extremely powerful engine the Reppu would not be able to challenge the new American fighters that were sure to emerge in the future. But the new engine I wanted to use had not been approved by the Navy, because in their eyes its development was not proceeding at an adequate pace. I also received an unofficial suggestion to replace the Zero's engine with the more powerful Mitsubishi "Kinsei" unit, but I could not evaluate and respond to this idea because of the serious lack of manpower in the design section.

I believe it happened about one o'clock in the afternoon of 18 April 1942. As I was struggling with the design of the Reppu, I thought I heard the sound of airplanes flying at low altitude. People in the design room were thrown into an uproar and were running toward the windows. At that moment, a twin-engine medium-sized bomber with stars on its wings flew over the plant. It dropped something which glittered. "An enemy airplane!" everyone screamed and looked out of the windows in time to see a streak of black smoke rising as we heard a loud explosion. The plane was a B–25 bomber and it had dropped a fire bomb. The damage was not too extensive, but the bombs did kill five employees and injure thirty others. Shortly thereafter, it was announced that both Tokyo and the Osaka-Kobe area had also been hit by B–25s. The raids were made by sixteen B–25s under the command of Lt. Col. James Doolittle; they had taken off from an aircraft carrier which slipped in close to Japan. This was the first air raid experienced by either Japan or myself!

Was the fighting getting this close? I could not help but feel gloomy about the future of the war. However, these bombings did not cause undue concern among the people and the reports of victories continued to be released.

In early June, when summer was creeping in slowly, a sea battle of unprecendented size was reported. This was the Battle of Midway, which was to be the turning point of the war. The newspaper headlines read, "We Stormed the Enemy Bases in the East Pacific," using the entire space of the top line, and reported the Imperial troops' victories along with advances in the Aleutians. According to the papers, the Americans lost two aircraft carriers and 120 airplanes while

Japan suffered the loss of only one carrier, had one carrier and one cruiser damaged, and had apparently lost 35 airplanes. With this kind of news, it was understandable that few people could gain insight into Japan's true fortunes. Only after the war was the truth made public: the results at Midway were just about opposite of what had been reported. The Americans lost one carrier and about 150 airplanes and 307 personnel, while Japan lost four principal carriers, 322 airplanes, and 3,500 personnel. I will not discuss the reasons for such a devastating defeat, since many have been offered including errors in scouting, strategy, and just plain bad luck, which seemed to follow us. Nonetheless, the Zero showed more fighting spirit during that battle than ever before. Indeed, perhaps that is why the pilots' spirits were so high.

Thirty-six Zeros escorted our attackers to Midway Island and gained complete supremacy by downing fifty enemy fighters in addition to protecting our attackers from the F4Fs and Buffalos which awaited us there. In the meantime, almost all of the enemy aircraft that attacked our carriers were shot down either by Zeros which were protecting the carriers or by the carriers themselves, and there was not a single hit made on our fleet. Then, as our first attackers returned from Midway, enemy bombers made their initial raids. Zeros fought and downed these enemy aircraft, using their last fuel reserves. Some Zeros landed, quickly refueled, and took off from the tossing decks as the carriers attempted to dodge enemy aircraft. The Zeros downed another seventy airplanes, which was almost the total number of American aircraft available for combat. But it became clear at the last moment that fortune had deserted the Japanese forces. The Japanese attackers returning from the first Midway strike landed on the carriers, and the second group which had been delayed because of tactical error was preparing to take off. Then without warning enemy carrier-based dive bombers came roaring through the clouds, and within minutes the Japanese carriers started to smoke as they caught fire. The battle ended all too soon. The Zeros in the air and the ships' anti-aircraft guns simply did not have time to discover the enemy aircraft and respond. The Zeros on the decks could not take off and were soon destroyed by fire. Thus, the Zeros fought well under the given conditions, but the entire operation had been risky from the beginning. Even as I write this, I feel pain for the tragedy of the Japanese Imperial Navy and the Zero fighter.

Meanwhile, in the Aleutian operation, which was conducted simultaneously and was reported to be a success much greater than it actually was, an unfortunate incident occurred. An almost undamaged Zero made a forced landing on an uninhabited island and the United States took possession of it. There was not a single person in Japan at the time who knew about this. Since Pearl Harbor, the United States had made many efforts to discover the secrets of our mysterious airplane, including an attempt to assemble pieces of downed aircraft into one flyable model. Now the Americans were able to conduct an investigation of Japan's newest fighter from all angles, using this almost perfect model for flight tests. They quickly learned the advantages and disadvantages of the Zero. The results of their investigation played a significant role in new fighter design and tactics to be used against our fighters.

A Campaign to Shoot Down Zeros

In August 1942, Mr. Kamijyo, a fellow employee of the Nagoya manufacturing plant, returned from New York aboard an alien exchange ship, and I was able to learn some inside facts about America. He told us the following story, saying he could tell it without hesitation, since he had related it three times previously, once at the military intelligence office, again at the main office of Mitsubishi, and finally at the Nagoya manufacturing plant. In the camp where he was held in America, newspapers were freely available. According to the papers, the Zeros were unquestionably strong and losses of American planes and pilots were high. Losses of American forces to bomber raids were also reported as serious. He also added that an astronomical increase in American military airplane production would soon take place and that a number of new designs specifically tailored to fight the Zero were steadily making progress.

The Japanese people began to take an optimistic view of the war as continued reports of victories were made and the fatal loss at Midway was withheld from the public. I, too, was encouraged by this triumphant atmosphere, although I still had my doubts. But after listening to Mr. Kamijyo, a cold shudder ran through my body, and the uncertainties I had felt at the beginning of the war suddenly came back. On the other hand, I learned what respect the Americans had for the Zero. I was thinking of the skies to the faraway south; as I listened to Mr. Kamijyo's talk, it seemed certain that the Zero would have tough battles ahead of it, since the Allies were developing a new plan to drive it from the skies.

Shortly after Mr. Kamijyo's return, newspapers ran a front-page story reporting that air and sea battles had taken place near the Solomon Islands in the South Pacific. At the time, I did not know this was the beginning of the operation to repossess Guadalcanal, which was the first step of an Allied counterattack. Soon after this news, during a meeting held at the Aeronautical Engineering Establishment, I was again asked to improve the Zero. This time, they wanted me to recover the loss of range and the decrease in dogfight performance suffered when we went to the Sakae engine with the two-stage supercharger and shortened the wing span fifty centimeters on each side by eliminating the rounded wing tips. In order to fulfill this request, we fitted an extra fuel tank in the outer wing and replaced the original tip. This enabled the airplane to cruise for one additional hour. In those days, the fleet of Zeros at Rabaul would take off from their base and escort attackers to Guadalcanal, but it was 1,050 kilometers between Guadalcanal and Rabaul, too far even for the Zeros with their present range capability. Hence, the improvement was requested in orders to allow the performance of this difficult mission. As I listened to the request, I thought, "The Zeros must be greatly overworked." Regrettably, with the additional fuel tank we had about reached the limit so far as range was concerned. With the new modifications, the Zero became the model 22 A6M3.

Fierce struggles took place over Guadalcanal between the United States and Japanese forces during the Battle of the Solomons, followed by the Second Battle of the Solomons, the Battle of the South Pacific, and the Third Battle of the Solomons. These operations received much attention in the papers, but I was apt to forget about the Zeros because I was so busy in designing the Reppu. The Reppu was nearing its completion stage and even the engine had been selected, although it was not the one I wanted to use. About this time, the United States completed its study of an anti-Zero policy, using the Zero it had obtained in the Aleutians. The new tactics developed during this study were first unveiled as the Americans fought the Battle of the Solomons. Usually, the new tactics were used by the F4F, which could not defeat the Zero if ordinary tactics were used. But now American pilots were instructed as follows: "Do not attempt to dogfight with the Zero unless you are in pairs. With two aircraft in a pair, strike the first blow by diving; if the Zero tries to drag you into a dogfight, protect each other's rear by flying crisscross and don't let the Zero come at you from the rear. Under all circumstances, dives should be halted at the proper time and you should maintain an altitude that does not give the Zero the opportunity to get behind you. Then you must wait for the next chance to attack." This was the famous "USATI" tactic.

In the fall of 1942, the United States introduced a new airplane in the Solomons campaign, the Lockheed P–38 Lightning, which was the first new American airplane put into combat since the F4F. It was a single-seat, twin-engine, twin-boom, high altitude fighter with three times the power of the Zero. It had superb high altitude performance, higher maximum speed, and higher dive speed than the Zero. However, as a rule, this type of fighter had a large turning radius and its maneuverability worsened as the speed decreased. The Zero could shoot it down easily if the enemy pilot was willing to dogfight, and at first Zero pilots gave it a contemptible nickname, *Pero-Hachi*. But as soon as P–38 pilots started to use the tactics of surprise attack and rapid separation, fully utilizing their high altitude performance and dive speed, shooting at bombers while diving by at terrific speed and flying away like a phantom, it became difficult for the Zeros to defeat them unless the P–38s were discovered early.

In March 1943, Chance Vought's F4U Corsair, which was the first single-engine fighter that was a good opponent for the Zero, was introduced into the Solomons campaign. This fighter, with a unique reversed gull wing, was inferior to the Zero in dogfight performance, range, low speed control, and visibility, but it had superior maximum speed, dive speed, and armament, and twice the power of the Zero. These features, combined with the new tactics being used, made the F4U much more effective than other Allied fighters. Although it was a Marine fighter, it was not used on carriers at this time, since it could not safely land on carrier decks. However, the Allies were able to utilize the airplane by establishing a sequence of land bases on the islands.[4]

The development of new tactics and fighters by the United States proved to be an effective way to defeat the Zero. The United States had discovered the Zero's weak points in diving speed, high altitude performance, and maximum speed, all of which were sacrificed to obtain maneuverability and range, given the Zero's small engine. When the Allies started to use their well-planned tactics, it became much more difficult for the Zero to shoot down enemy aircraft.

We had only the Zero to fight against these new American aircraft as they were introduced one after the other. Naturally, the completion of the Raiden, which was to be responsible for air defense over our bases, was to be desired, but it was delayed time after time because of inadequate engine performance and insufficient design manpower. Without new aircraft, we had no other way to deal with the enemy except to continue to use improved versions of the Zero. So, in order to increase the maximum and dive speeds of the Zero, the wing span was once again decreased, this time to eleven meters, and a thrust-type augmentation system, which blew the engine exhaust to the rear at high speed, was adopted in place of the old manifold system. As a result of this, maximum level speed was raised to 565 km/hr, which was 20 km/hr faster than previous models. This was the Zero model 52, of which more were produced than any other model.

---

4. Translators' note: The F4U was initially restricted from carrier operations because it had a tendency to bounce upon landing. After its landing gear was redesigned, the F4U was cleared for carrier operations. In the Japanese edition of this book, it was stated that the F4U could not operate from American carriers since the carriers' decks were too short. We believe this is incorrect and have therefore modified the English-language edition.

According to the pilots who flew this model, dogfight performance declined because of the smaller wing area. Japan could not produce the model 52 in time for the Battle of Guadalcanal, and finally the nine-month-old battle came to an end with Japan's defeat. The United States' overwhelming strength in production and logistics had, at last, turned the tide. In February 1943, Japan withdrew over 10,000 officers and men from Guadalcanal; the withdrawal was reported in the papers as an "advancement," and this defeat was kept secret from the Japanese public.

As for the Navy Air Corps, perhaps in terms of technique they won the Guadalcanal battle, but they certainly lost it in terms of power. Mr. Minoru Genda wrote of the atmosphere of those days in the *Story of the Naval Air Corps* as follows:

> Since the beginning of the war, the Navy's Zero fighter force terrorized the enemy, and the name of the Zero won worldwide fame. In some cases, the enemy would retreat if they even saw the sign of a Zero. For the Rabaul Zero fighter force, which advanced to the skies of Guadalcanal, 560 nautical miles away, it was normal to control the air for as long as one hour at a time. During the all-out attack on Guadalcanal in the latter part of October 1942, Japan commanded complete air supremacy as long as our Zeros were in the air over the area. Some Naval transports were damaged, since the Zeros did not continuously control the skies because of the distance they had to fly and because of the small number of airplanes available, but this can hardly be blamed on the Zero's ability. Rather, it depended on the number of airplanes and the war situation.

Furthermore, Japan was forced to use mostly naval aircraft against the well-balanced forces of American Army and Navy planes, and during the air battles, the U.S. airplanes far outnumbered ours, as Mr. Genda pointed out.

In addition, a new problem faced us; frankly admitting the superior performance of the Zero, the United States concentrated its efforts on introducing a new fighter which could take air supremacy away from us, and also on completing a strategic bomber which would stop war production in Japan. There were clear indications which showed that the United States suspended development of other interim aircraft. In fact, even though new fighters were produced one after the other, the Allies were still using old models of single-engine carrier-based attackers and bombers. They also continued to use twin-engine and four-engine land-based bombers which had been in use at the start of the war, while their strategic bombers made remarkable developments from the B–17 to the B–29.

In Japan, where there was a shortage of engineering manpower, we found it took us twice as long to develop a new airplane, or even to redesign a current airplane, as it would take the Americans. Japan should have changed the national policy of priorities when the war started, but even two years later aircraft development was still carried out according to the same policies as it always had been. How can one explain the apparent lack of understanding of total war among the military authorities and politicians when it was they who had initiated the war against the United States? Such poor management of technical policy created the situation where we had no other choice but to rely on Zeros from the beginning of the war until its end, and this, in turn, accelerated Japan's decisive defeat.

15 August 1945

THE NEW RIVAL

In September 1943 there suddenly appeared a frightening new rival for the Zero, which was still effectively fighting in the slowly changing tide of war. The United States Navy's new fighter, the F6F Hellcat, first made its appearance during the sea battle near the Gilbert Islands, south of the Marshall Islands.

The F6F was similar to the F4U in that it had almost twice the power of the Zero; it was armed with six 12.7-mm machine guns and had self-sealing fuel tanks. It was more maneuverable than other U.S. fighters, and had a large wing area suitable for a carrier-based fighter. In addition, its top speed was slightly greater than that of the Zero. A fighter that could fight straight in the Zero's face had finally appeared in the United States' arsenal. America put tremendous emphasis on the F6F and, with the slogan "Down with the Zeros," hastened the aircraft into production as soon as its short flight test program was finished. Before long, F6F fighters were being delivered to the front lines in large quantities. With the participation of the F6F in battle, the Zero began its greatest ordeal. It was not simply a question of superior F6F performance; actually the Zero still had a chance to win in a one-to-one dogfight. But our maneuverability advantage was clearly getting smaller; our old tactic of replacing quantity with quality had reached its limit. At the same time, Japan had lost hundreds of her most skillful pilots in the defeats at Midway and Guadalcanal. To deal with this situation, it was necessary either to introduce a new, high quality fighter into combat or to increase the number of Zeros available for combat so as to reduce the quantity advantage the Americans now had. But the Raiden still needed a considerable amount of time before it would be ready for battle. The design of the Reppu, which was to improve on the Zero, was delayed because of the lack of a reliable powerful engine and a shortage of design manpower. Since the beginning of the war, the quantitative advantage of the United States over Japan was obvious, but now it clearly appeared that the difference in quality also favored the Americans. The fate of battle had moved to the sky. Hadn't Japan demonstrated to the world that it was far more important to secure air superiority by utilizing outstanding fighters rather than to increase the level of excellence of other types of aircraft which performed missions below the fighters' protective screen? To my regret, this lesson was learned by the United States rather than by us.

Thus, the United States moved her early fighters, the P–40 and the F4F, to the sidelines and started to send P–38s, F4Us, and F6Fs in quantity to the front lines. The Zeros were forced to face all of these new fighters alone. It was a tragic sight to see the Zeros, which had fought many battles since the beginning of the war, charging into the midst of these new enemy aircraft. Even more tragically, these Zeros we built with such painstaking effort were shot down one after the other in a shower of bullets fired from the six 12.7-mm machine guns mounted on the F6F.

One Improvement after the Other

People who understood the situation in those days must have thought, "This is serious. Something must be done." The Navy officials with whom I associated began to show signs of impatience when the development of the Zero's successor fell behind schedule. As a simple and effective measure, there was only one solution—to revise the Zero by improving its performance. A large-scale redesign, such as replacing the Sakae power plant with a more powerful unit, could not be officially initiated unless a decision were made to change the distribution of design team manpower. Under these circumstances, small redesigns of the Zero continued at a fast pace. An automatic fire extinguisher for the internal fuel tanks was added to the model 52. This aircraft also had a higher top speed and greater rolling speed during dogfights than did the model 22. Next, the number of shells for the 20-mm cannons was increased and the cannons were re-designed to have a higher rate of fire in the model 52a. On the model 52b, one 13-mm machine gun replaced the two 7.7-mm guns, and a bulletproof windshield and automatic fire extinguishers were added for the fuselage fuel tank. On the model 52c, two 13-mm machine guns were added in the wing, replacing the 7.7-mm machine guns, and four rockets were also fitted under the wings. In addition, a bulletproof bulkhead was installed in the rear of the cockpit and a self-sealing bulletproof fuel tank was added behind this.

No matter how the government tried to distort the news, these requests for redesign clearly told the story of the Zero's ordeal and the difficult situation Japan faced. The most significant request was for bulletproofing, a feature which had not even been mentioned in the Zero's initial planning requirements. Over the years, the lack of bulletproofing has frequently been mentioned as a weak point of the Zero. The reason for this shortcoming was that the aircraft could not afford the additional weight necessary for bulletproofing, given the requirements stipulated with respect to heavy armament, long-range capability, and maneuverability. These items took priority over anything else, and since we did not have reliable high-power engines, bulletproofing was sacrificed. Japanese pilots of those days had a feeling similar to that which must have been experienced by skillful samurai who singlehandedly fought many well-protected ene-mies. This attitude on the part of the pilots accelerated the general trend of assigning a low priority to bulletproofing. Certainly, if one type of aircraft demonstrated overwhelming offensive ability, this in itself could become a major defensive force. But as our op-ponents' offensive abilities approached or even exceeded our own, an unskilled pilot or one who was outnumbered needed the additional protection of bulletproofing.

The sight of Zeros taking off carrying unsuitable bulletproofing and extra firearms surely indicated Japan's future in this war. As the war progressed, the United States isolated Rabaul, one of Japan's most important bases in the south, and rendered it powerless. It became obvious that America was following the strategy of heading directly north toward the Japanese home islands while taking over other Japanese bases one after the other. At this point, Japan's prospects in the war were clearly sagging.

Earlier, I stated that for Japan the biggest obstacle in airplane production was the short supply of raw materials. Shipments of raw materials from the south clearly started to decrease about this time. This was caused by enemy submarine interference with our supply routes. Back home, we were striving to increase production under the slogan, "One hundred million in unison," but after reaching a peak in the summer of 1944, production started to decline rapidly because of insufficient materials and a lack of manpower. On top of this, the Marianas had fallen, and since the Americans had constructed a big base there, they were able to start full-scale B–29 attacks on the home islands. Then, suddenly, every activity in Japan was slowed down, not just airplane production; misfortune seldom acts alone. On 7 December 1944, a strong earthquake shook the Nagoya area killing nearly 1,000 people. At the factories of Mitsubishi and Aichi, which were built on soft landfills, the concrete floors cracked and important jigs, in which airplanes were assembled, became misaligned and some buildings were destroyed.

While we were correcting the misalignment of the jigs, a formation of B–29s bombed Mitsubishi's engine plant on 13 December and Mitsubishi's and Aichi's airframe plants on 18 December. I was at the Mitsubishi plant during the air raid and took shelter in a vacant lot just outside the buildings when I heard the siren's piercing cry. As I lay face down in the ditch, I looked up out of the corner of my eyes toward the roaring sound and saw a column of more than ten beautiful B–29s leisurely approaching at an altitude of about 10,000 meters. I tensed my shoulders at the sharp noise of the bombs falling through the air, and heard explosions. The raid inflicted heavy casualties at the engine plant; it was clear that this was the prelude to the full-scale bombing of the home islands. The government, which was caught between the conflicting requirements of increased production and industrial dispersion, finally decided to carry out the emergency evacuation of all aircraft plants and other major plants. It was in this atmosphere that the Raiden was finally accepted, but it was not introduced at the front lines in quantity, because it still had some problems such as poor visibility and excessive vibration. We changed the engine in the Reppu to the one I had originally wanted to use; it then became the "reincarnation of the Zero." But its flight tests and additional prototype production made slow progress. People donated whatever metal products they could in the hope that "one more airplane could be built." We also collected pine roots and grew castor oil plants in hopes of relieving the shortage of fuel and lubricants. But even such painful nationwide efforts were in vain.

KAMIKAZE

In the latter part of October 1944, the existence of the Kamikaze Special Attack Forces was reported in the newspapers with headlines stating, "Imperial Pilots Launch Desperate Sacrifice Attacks on the Enemy Fleet." Earlier, in June, when I learned that the Mariana Islands had fallen, I thought the fate of Japan was sealed. Now, reading this article, I said to myself, "Finally we have been driven this far!" In the months that followed, many reports of the special forces attacks on enemy fleets were made public. I guessed from the articles that these operations were decided by frontline officers without waiting for approval from headquarters, as a last vain effort to fend off the American invasion of the Philippine Islands. I cried in my heart when I thought of the pitiful Japanese Samurai forced to face a much too powerful enemy but unable to withdraw even if he wanted to do so; instead, he must sacrifice himself. Soon I also learned that Zeros were being utilized as Kamikaze attack aircraft. Then, on 23 November 1944, the name Zero was made public for the first time, as a "newly unveiled fighter," as if to encourage the people of Japan, who by that time were exhausted by the war and were becoming desperate.

After reaching this point in my story, I pulled out and read an essay which I once wrote entitled "Compliment to the Kamikaze Special Attack Forces." When the publishing bureau of the *Asahi* newspaper's main office in Osaka was preparing to publish the book "Kamikaze Special Attack Forces" in December of 1944, they asked ten people with various backgrounds to each write a short essay, and I was one of them. But I was not able to devote much time to the essay, since I was so busy with my normal work. Many young men with bright futures made the sacrifice attacks where there was no hope of return. According to the papers, they boarded their aircraft with their lips sealed and silent smiles on their faces. At first, I could not write anything, because it wrenched my heart to think of the scene. The aircraft these brave young men boarded with smiles were Zeros.

Finally, encouraging myself, I started to write, telling myself I would write my words for those who lost their loved ones in the war. But as I started writing, I could not stop tears from running down my cheeks. About a month later, during the New Year holidays of 1945, I finished the essay. Its first words were, "I respectfully respond." It was impossible for me to praise the special attackers without qualifications. Why did Japan plunge into a war she could not expect to win? Why were the Zeros used in such a way? These questions hovered in my mind. Of course, I could not say such things publicly at that time, but I strongly wished to include at least a paragraph of protest, as follows: "The strength of the enemy is endless, but our productivity is limited. We have reached the limits of human intelligence and have selfishly tried all kinds of methods to make effective adjustments to our limited human and material resources so that new arms could emerge. As I have witnessed the birth of the Zero, I know there is nothing to fear, since we have created an aircraft worthy of its task and the Kamikaze Special Attack Forces to do the job that must be done." The feelings I concealed in these words were very complicated. The true meaning is, if we had done what we should have done, we might have been able to avoid such an awful thing as the Special Attack Forces.

THE END OF THE WAR

In 1945, the B–29 raids were intensified during January, February, and March. The formations of B–29s dropped tons of bombs as they flew by unopposed at high altitudes and were frequently seen over Nagoya; apparently the airframe and engine plants had the highest priority for bombing. Once I saw an Army fighter in the sky above me heroically attack and crash into a B–29 bomber while the air raid sirens screamed. In that lone Army fighter, I saw the image of the Zero still fighting desperately in the South Pacific.

Luckily, my house did not receive any damage from the bombings, but on the way home I saw many places in town burned down. Often smoke was rising to high altitudes where contrails could still be seen showing the location of earlier dogfights. Mitsubishi began to disperse its operation according to airplane type and we in the engineering division, including the prototype plant, relocated to the Nagano and Matsumoto districts. My family and I moved to Matsumoto in May 1945. People in other industrial plants also started to disperse about the same time. Transportation and communication systems had been disrupted, which had an unsettling effect on all of us. The completion of new plant facilities took a long time; as materials and parts became harder to obtain, production naturally came to a standstill. Even if we had the will to work, during those difficult times we had little with which to work. Production of Zeros at the Mitsubishi plant was no less than one hundred units per month during November 1944, but in July 1945 we were able to produce only fifteen units.

Judging from conditions on the home front, the end of the war was imminent. At noon on 15 August 1945, I heard His Majesty's voice on the radio as I sat in my rented house in the suburb of Matsumoto. Summer in Matsumoto is sizzling hot, and after returning home from my office via bicycle that day under the burning rays of the sun, I had washed myself with a cold towel. I usually went home for lunch, and earlier in the day it had been announced there would be a special broadcast at noon. The landlord, his wife, and I all gathered in front of the radio without bothering to have lunch.

His Majesty's grave voice was audible only about half of the time because of recording noise, but we quickly realized he was announcing that the war was over. As we sat there with our heads drooping, trying to hold back tears, each of us was filled with emotion but none had the strength to speak. I thought, "This finishes the job to which I have devoted one half of my life." At the same time, I felt disappointment even though I was now relieved of the ordeal and stress of the past few years. Would this end my association with aircraft? Such a thought made me sad. We had had unregrettable days during the last ten years, but in the meantime what foolish steps Japan had taken! Perhaps Japan was not the only fool, but she had lost millions of invaluable lives, not to mention the wasted efforts and assets of those who survived. My first thought was that our losses were the result of poor political leadership caused by a lack of consideration and responsibility. I prayed, "Let intelligent leaders step forward."

THE ZERO STILL LIVES

What I experienced during the postwar period was common to all Japanese. When I look back, many unforgettable memories come to me, mixed in with recollections of mental and physical hardships even greater than those of the war. Within less than twenty years after the war, Japan was successfully reconstructed from the ruins, and today she is prospering materially as if there had never been a war. There are no storms around me now, and the few years I spent in long agony and short joy with the Zero and other airplanes are bygone dreams.

However, for me, the experience of those years provided a number of valuable lessons and became the foundation on which I tried to live during the postwar period. Since my childhood, I have been rather shy and poor at talking and have only been good at solving problems. I have never liked arguments without substantiation and do not like arguments for the sake of argument. I have always believed that I should show actual results and not just make noise. As I handled the difficult jobs of the Prototype 7 fighter, the Type 96 fighter, and the Zero fighter, I acted on this belief, which is fundamental for a technically-oriented man.

Unlike the imaginative work of an artist, the task of an engineer is always shadowed by severe, realistic conditions and requirements. But in order to achieve a high quality of creativity within this framework, the engineer must use free imagination to crack through ordinary paths of thinking, and this must be coupled with complete rationality. If the given package cannot be altered in any way, and if only ordinary ideas are employed, little difference will be achieved between final products. During the design of the Zero and other airplanes, I was deeply engrossed in the problem at hand, but I had to constantly keep in mind that it was necessary to go one step beyond the normal limits of thinking within the given conditions. I think the Zero is a good symbolic example of what can be achieved by thinking "one step beyond." There is of course no perfect victory in the battle against severe requirements. Critics have pointed to various weaknesses of the Zero, but when a technical evaluation is made, unless the various given conditions are carefully considered, the truth may not be found. I think we should not forget this when discussing the apparent shortcomings of the Zero. Aeronautical engineer Ichiro Naito discussed this briefly in the magazine *Maru* in June 1963: "acknowledging the Zero was an excellent airplane, from time to time I hear criticisms of inadequate strength and power, lack of bulletproofing, insufficient high altitude performance, etc. Many of these statements are only wild fantasies which come from partial knowledge. But, even if they were all true, I want you to think it over. Where in the world presently or in the past did an airplane exist which was as good as the Zero powered by an engine which barely delivered 1,000 horsepower?"

The following may be an unnecessary addition to the above comments, but most of the Zero's problems can be traced to its underpowered engine. I have already mentioned bulletproofing. In other respects, too, our basic dilemma was that we had to compete in performance with the world's best fighters, although our engines were always 20 to 30 percent less powerful than those of the more advanced countries. Therefore, it became impossible to satisfy all requirements across the board, and it was necessary to assign priorities and design the airplane accordingly. In Japan, this procedure was well established, perhaps more so than in other countries. From this point of view, it was natural for a fighter not to be bulletproofed. However, priorities varied between different aircraft types. For example, a bomber could not maneuver to avoid the bullets of an enemy fighter in daytime combat, regardless of its top speed. Consequently, bulletproofing should have been a high priority item for a bomber. In fact, the Type 1 land-based attack bomber was manufactured without utilizing the lessons learned from the Type 96 land-based attacker, which had suffered much damage during the early part of the Second Sino-Japanese War. The Type 1 had to be fitted with an awkward-looking self-sealing fuel tank early in the Pacific war. But in the case of a fighter, the pilot's skill and the performance of the airplane could compensate for the lack of bulletproofing to some extent. In short, bulletproofing was a low priority for a fighter, but it became more important as pilot skill decreased and as the number of enemy fighters increased. To corroborate this, the following comments are offered.

A document entitled "Reference Information for Planning of Future Fighters," compiled by the Navy Aeronautics Headquarters one year and five months after the beginning of the war, had this to say: "The Zero's performance, in general, is excellent. As it is, the Zero is by no means inferior to existing American fighters in the south Pacific, including the F4U . . . *even for a fighter* it will be necessary to include bulletproofing in the future." In those days, the consensus still seemed to be that the advantages of improved maneuverability and increased offensive firepower with a lighter aircraft made it inadvisable to weigh a fighter down with bulletproofing. In the future, bulletproofing would clearly be necessary, but for the present its absence resulted from our efforts to strengthen offensive firepower. As a matter of fact, only when the United States stepped up the counterattack and introduced new, powerful fighters in overwhelming numbers did bulletproofing become essential.

Next, let us look at speed and, in particular, insufficient dive speed. If the most suitable wing area were selected to accomplish the missions of air supremacy, escort, and attack, with a 1,000 horsepower engine, it would be impossible to obtain a speed higher than the Zero's. Only God could have done so. As proof of this, there has never existed anywhere in the world a fighter powered by a 1,000 hp air-cooled engine that was faster than the Zero, even without comparable range and dogfight characteristics.

So far as insufficient high altitude performance is concerned, it is asking too much for a carrier-based fighter, which is restricted in landing and takeoff field lengths, to perform as well as the regular, high altitude interceptors used by the Allies during the second half of the war. Fighters specifically designed as high altitude interceptors had more powerful superchargers than the two-stage blower used on the Zero model 32; they were fitted with either an exhaust-driven unit or a mechanical multistage type.

It is very difficult to judge the merits of different aircraft by making direct comparisons. For example, an accurate assessment of comparative industrial strengths can be made only if two countries' end products were conceived and produced during the same time period. It is not so simple if the products are not from the same era. Above all, in the fields of aircraft and automobiles, especially aircraft, it is standard procedure to equip later models with more powerful engines, a custom which reflects advancing technology. For this reason, later models are often much more effective than their predecessors. A meaningful comparison can be made only by analyzing two airplanes item by item and deciding which improvements were the result of improved technology and which were the result of better or more clever ideas.

In the case of airplanes active during the war, the ratio of victories per number of airplanes produced can approximately show the true value of the airplane. Of course, to judge an airplane like the Zero, which fought for five years with a power increase of less than 10 percent, we must separate its life into two parts. In the first half it was fighting against its own class, whereas in the second it was up against a generation of newer, heavier fighters. The production of Zeros continued until the last day of the war. Mitsubishi and Nakajima together produced a total of approximately 10,425 airplanes.

I think the method suggested above has merit, since it can also be used to assess general merchandise. New products compete with other products manufactured during the same time period, and only those that incorporate good ideas and are well timed can be successful. The value of competitive ideas and timing can be understood only by analyzing the characteristics of the products and estimating the environment and industrial capability of the competition. To succeed, a new concept must be beyond the knowledge of most experts or the trend of the times. It must be introduced ahead of its competitors and be supported by knowledge ahead of, and not just in conformity with, the times. Only under such circumstances can the developing countries compete with the advanced nations. If we do not bear this in mind, our products may approach the world's top quality level, but equaling or exceeding it will always be beyond our grasp.

There are people who say the Japanese lack ideas and are handy only at copying, but I never believed this was true. I hesitate to speak for the Zero, but even today people not only in Japan but from other parts of the world still talk of their admiration of the Zero and its abilities. For instance, Mr. J. W. Fozard, chief planning designer of the Hawker Aircraft Company, wrote in the November 1958 issue of the *Journal Of the Royal Aeronautical Society*, as follows:

Conditioned as most of us are to the popular view that the Japanese engineer excels more in copying than in creating, it is rather a shock to learn how advanced their aircraft technology became. For example, in 1940, after the loss of the second prototype Zero, the Naval Aircraft Establishment flew simulated combat sorties in Zero aircraft fitted with g-recorders to obtain a statistical loading spectrum. This data was then used to estimate the wing spar fatigue life and to form the basis for a programme of repeated-loading tests on Zero main spars. Further, it was the failure in flight of an early production Zero which led to the development of reliable dynamically similar wing models for wind tunnel flutter tests as early as 1941. But perhaps the most astonishing technological ingenuity, by Western standards, was the use in the Zero, and later fighters, of deliberate flexibility in the elevator circuit in order to increase the stick movement per g at high indicated airspeeds.[1]

1. J. W. Fozard, "Book Reviews," *Journal of the Royal Aeronautical Society* 62 (November 1958) : 839–40.

An interesting investigation concerning control response was conducted in the United States in 1962 to 1963 when Cornell Aeronautical Laboratory studied the characteristics of the pilot-preferred control system, the system that matches the pilot's control response using simulators. The results were identical to those I had obtained and used to design the Zero's control system nearly twenty years earlier.

In 1963, Adm. George W. Anderson, chief of naval operations for the United States during the hearings of the Senate Permanent Investigations Subcommittee, said:

> If a potential enemy either believes or knows his prospective adversary possesses such an edge, he thinks twice before committing himself to armed conflict. If other considerations compel him to act, this edge can make the all-important difference between being able to defeat the aggressor, or blunting his attack while production and manpower can be mobilized, or, lacking the edge, loosing quickly. The latter alternative being unacceptable, we must insure this edge is available to us. As a one inch longer reach is to a boxer, this edge is often very small when measured in terms such as altitude, miles per hour, range, time on station, operating depths and the like. The Japanese Zero initially enjoyed an edge in maneuverability—small, but most serious in terms of pilots killed, aircraft lost and ships sunk by the torpedo planes and bombers the Zeros escorted.[2]

There have been many famous airplanes in the history of aviation, but this reference to the Zero made in this official context after more than twenty years shows the strong impression it must have had on the experts in the Allied countries during the war.

In his book *Famous Fighters of the Second World War*, English critic William Green wrote as follows:

> To the Japanese the Zero-sen was everything that the Spitfire was to the British nation. It symbolized Japan's conduct of the war, for as its fortune fared so fared the Japanese nation. The Zero fighter marked the beginning of a new epoch in naval aviation: it was the first shipboard

2. *Aviation Week and Space Technology*, 15 April 1963.

fighter capable of besting its land-based opponents. It created a myth—
the myth of Japanese invincibility in the air, and one to which the
Japanese themselves fell victim as a result of the almost total destruction of Allied airpower in the early days of the Pacific war. In its day
the Zero was the world's foremost carrier-based fighter, and its appearance over Pearl Harbour came as a complete surprise to the American
forces. Its successive appearance over every major battle area in the
opening days of the war seemed to indicate that Japan possessed un-
limited supplies of this remarkable fighter, and its almost mystical
powers of maneuver and ability to traverse vast stretches of water fos-
tered the acceptance of the myth of its invincibility in Allied minds.[3]

I was very touched to hear the words of Mr. Fozard, Admiral Anderson, and Mr. Green, since they came from former opponents who
had lost many lives, airplanes, and ships because of the Zero fighter.

There are scholars in Japan who criticize as follows: "Admittedly,
Japan had excellent final products such as the Zero, but we were
dependent upon advanced countries for the basic knowledge and did
not ourselves conduct basic research." I admit there is some truth in
this, because Japan had not yet completely caught up with the advanced countries of the world in regard to aeronautical science. It is
not a question of good or bad, but rather a matter of course. When
a country becomes advanced in all fields, it is not necessary to
depend on others for knowledge. But, in reality, the rule of economy
says, if knowledge has been developed in any country, it is sound
policy for all of mankind to borrow it, cultivate certain aspects of it,
and share the knowledge obtained with others. In the process of
improving a product, research frequently reveals new knowledge. I
believe this was also true in the case of the Zero.

Thus, many people in Japan and the rest of the world now know
that our endless efforts and creative insights in those days bore beautiful fruit—the Zero fighter. I believe that the technical traditions and
engineering spirit which created the Zero still exist among Japanese.
Many of my colleagues who shared the same pleasures and hardships

3. William Green, *Famous Fighters of the Second World War*, rev. ed. (New
York: Doubleday and Company, 1976), p. 64.

in those days are still working to further the progress of Japan's technology in general, and not just in aviation. It is a great pleasure for me to know that the Zero fighter, to which I devoted half of my life, is still alive today, not only in our technology, but also in the hearts of the people of Japan.

Index